DAVE THOMAS

DAVE THOMAS

Nancy Peacock

Introduction by James Scott Brady,
Trustee, the Center to Prevent Handgun Violence
Vice Chairman, the Brain Injury Foundation

Chelsea House Publishers
Philadelphia

CHELSEA HOUSE PUBLISHERS

EDITOR IN CHIEF Stephen Reginald
PRODUCTION MANAGER Pamela Loos
ART DIRECTOR Sara Davis
DIRECTOR OF PHOTOGRAPHY Judy L. Hasday
MANAGING EDITOR James D. Gallagher

Staff for **Dave Thomas**
ASSOCIATE ART DIRECTOR Takeshi Takahashi
DESIGNER Keith Trego
PICTURE RESEARCHER Sandy Jones

COVER ILLUSTRATION Ismael Roldan

The Chelsea House World Wide Web site address is:
www.chelseahouse.com

First Printing

1 3 5 7 9 8 6 4 2

Library of Congress Cataloging-in-Publication Data

Peacock, Nancy.
Dave Thomas / by Nancy Peacock

p. cm. — (Overcoming adversity)
Includes bibliographical references and index
Summary: A biography of the man who founded Wendy's, one of the nation's largest restaurant chains.

ISBN 0-7910-5302-4. — ISBN 0-7910-5303-2 (pbk.)
1. Thomas, R. David, 1932–   Juvenile literature. 2. Restaurateurs—United States Biography Juvenile literature. 3. Wendy's International Juvenile literature.
[1. Thomas, R. David, 1932–   . 2. Restaurateurs. 3. Wendy's International.]
I. Title. II. Series.
TX910.5.T56P43   1999
338.7'616479573—dc21
[B]   99–31495
                                                             CIP

CONTENTS

OVERCOMING ADVERSITY

TIM ALLEN
comedian/performer

MAYA ANGELOU
author

APOLLO 13 MISSION
astronauts

LANCE ARMSTRONG
professional cyclist

DREW BARRYMORE
actress

JAMES BRADY
gun control activist

DREW CAREY
comedian/performer

JIM CARREY
comedian/performer

BILL CLINTON
U.S. president

TOM CRUISE
actor

MICHAEL J. FOX
actor

WHOOPI GOLDBERG
comedian/performer

EKATERINA GORDEEVA
figure skater

SCOTT HAMILTON
figure skater

JEWEL
singer and poet

JAMES EARL JONES
actor

QUINCY JONES
musician and producer

ABRAHAM LINCOLN
U.S. president

WILLIAM PENN
Pennsylvania's founder

JACKIE ROBINSON
baseball legend

ROSEANNE
entertainer

MONICA SELES
tennis star

SAMMY SOSA
baseball star

DAVE THOMAS
entrepreneur

SHANIA TWAIN
entertainer

ROBIN WILLIAMS
performer

STEVIE WONDER
entertainer

ON FACING ADVERSITY

James Scott Brady

I GUESS IT'S a long way from a Centralia, Illinois, train yard to the George Washington University Hospital Trauma Unit. My dad was a yardmaster for the old Chicago, Burlington & Quincy Railroad. As a child, I used to get to sit in the engineer's lap and imagine what it was like to drive that train. I guess I always have liked being in the "driver's seat."

Years later, however, my interest turned from driving trains to driving campaigns. In 1979, former Texas governor John Connally hired me as a press secretary in his campaign for the American presidency. We lost the Republican primary to a former Hollywood star named Ronald Reagan. But I managed to jump over to the Reagan campaign. When Reagan was elected in 1980, I was "sitting in the catbird seat," as humorist James Thurber would say—poised to be named presidential press secretary. I held that title throughout the eight years of the Reagan administration. But not without one terrible, extended interruption.

It happened barely two months after the Reagan administration took office. I never even heard the shots. On March 30, 1981, my life went blank in an instant. In an attempt to assassinate President Reagan, John Hinckley Jr. armed himself with a "Saturday night special"—a low-quality, $29 pistol—and shot wildly as our presidential entourage exited a Washington hotel. One of the exploding bullets struck me just above the left eye. It shattered into a couple dozen fragments, some of which penetrated my skull and entered my brain.

The next few months of my life were a nightmare of repeated surgery, broken contact with the outside world, and a variety of medical complications. More than once, I was very close to death.

The next few years were filled with frustrating struggles to function with a paralyzed right side, struggles to speak and communicate.

To people who face and defeat daunting obstacles, "ambition" is not becoming wealthy or famous or winning elections or awards. Words like "ambition" and "achievement" and "success" take on very different meanings. The objective is just to live, to wake up every morning. The goals are not lofty; they are very ordinary.

My own heroes are ordinary folks—but they accomplish extraordinary things because they try. My greatest hero is my wife, Sarah. She's accomplished a lot of things in life, but two stand out. The first has been the way she has cared for me and our son since I was shot. A tremendous tragedy and burden was dropped unexpectedly into her life, totally beyond her control and without justification. She could have given up; instead, she focused her energies on preserving our family and returning our lives to normal as much as possible. Week by week, month by month, year by year, she has not reached for the miraculous, just for the normal. Yet in focusing on the normal, she has helped accomplish the miraculous.

Her other most remarkable accomplishment, to me, has been spearheading the effort to keep guns out of the hands of criminals and children in America. Opponents call her a "gun grabber"; I call her a national hero. And I am not alone.

After a seven-year battle, during which Sarah and I worked tirelessly to educate the public about the need for stronger gun laws, the Brady Bill became law in 1993. It was a victory, achieved in the face of tremendous opposition, that now benefits all Americans. From the time the law took effect through fall 1997, background checks had stopped 173,000 criminals and other high-risk purchasers from buying handguns, and the law has helped to reduce illegal gun trafficking.

Sarah was not pursuing fame, or even recognition. She simply started at one point—when our son, Scott, found a loaded handgun on the seat of a pickup truck and, thinking it was a toy, pointed it at Sarah.

Fortunately, no one was hurt. But seeing a gun nearly bring a second tragedy upon our family, Sarah became determined to do whatever she could to prevent senseless death and injury from guns.

Some people think of Sarah as a powerful political force. To me, she's the person who so many times fed me and helped me dress during my long years of recovery.

Overcoming obstacles is part of life, not just for people who are challenged by disabilities, illnesses, or tragedies, but for all people. No matter what the obstacle—fear, disability, prejudice, grief, or a difficulty that isn't likely to "just go away"—we can all work to make this world a better place.

Dave Thomas poses with talk show host Rosie O'Donnell next to a large picture of the first commemorative postage stamp celebrating adoption. Dave was devastated when he learned at age 13 that he had been adopted; today, the founder of Wendy's is an advocate for adopted children, participating in events that raise awareness of adoption issues.

1

A DEVASTATING
DISCOVERY

Adopted.

The word filled Dave's mind with a mixture of anger and fear.

Adopted? Why hadn't anyone told him before? But now his grandmother was saying that his parents had adopted him shortly after his birth in 1932.

"When Grandma Minnie told me that I was adopted, I felt my stomach turn and I was really afraid," Dave recalled years later. "Then I was angry that no one had told me sooner."

It wasn't as though life had been a bed of roses for Dave up to that point. At the age of 13, Dave Thomas was a young man who had spent most of his life yearning for something he did not have: a loving home and two parents who cared about him.

Dave's only memory of his mother, Auleva Thomas, was when he visited her once in the hospital. She died soon after Dave's visit, when he was only five years old. Dave's father, Rex Thomas, was a gruff, distant man who remarried several times and moved his ever-increasing family from town to town, looking for work. The country was still in the grip of the Great Depression, and good jobs were hard to find.

After his mother's death Dave's grandmother explained to him that his mother had gone to heaven, where she would watch over him. Dave accepted her explanation; there wasn't too much else a five-year-old boy could do.

For 13-year-old Dave, finding out that he was adopted was the ultimate betrayal in a life already filled with pain and loneliness. Growing up with a father who never bothered to hide his indifference and disapproval only made Dave's sense of abandonment worse.

He couldn't know it at that awful moment, but life held much better things in store for Dave Thomas. Even though he had very little to show for it yet, Dave was already developing an ability to work hard and dream big. These abilities would help make Dave become one of the most successful businessmen in modern restaurant history.

As a young man Dave had one enormous advantage going for him: his grandma Minnie Sinclair. She recognized her grandson's need for her love and support, and she gave him an endless supply of both. "She sensed my frustration and resentment and really went out of her way to make me feel good about myself," Dave says in his autobiography, *Dave's Way.*

Dave found other special people besides his grandmother, usually his employers and coworkers. They saw in Dave a bright, sensitive young man who desperately wanted to succeed. Dave wanted to prove to his dad—and to himself—that he truly was somebody special.

Today Dave Thomas's name is a household word, and his face is seen on TV commercials around the world. Over the course of the last 30 years he has turned a hamburger restaurant called Wendy's in downtown Columbus, Ohio, into a $6-billion international business, with more than 5,000 stores in over 30 different countries.

His childhood began in poverty and loneliness, but he grew up to play golf with presidents and celebrities and eat dinner at the White House. And since 1990, when he was asked by President George Bush to be the spokesperson for a national campaign to raise adoption awareness, he has turned the stigma of adoption into a national cause.

Dave would be the first to admit that it took a lifetime of hard work to make it happen.

A family sits down to a home-cooked lunch—hamburgers, Dave Thomas's favorite meal.
When he was a child, Dave and his father often ate in restaurants instead of at home.

2

A KID
IN BETWEEN

DAVE THOMAS WAS born on July 2, 1932, in Atlantic City, a popular beach resort on the coast of New Jersey. He never knew his birth parents; he was adopted by a young couple from Kalamazoo, Michigan, Rex and Auleva Thomas.

Dave's earliest memories are of his mother Auleva's death from rheumatic fever. Rheumatic fever has a number of symptoms: high fever, swelling, aching joints, and inflamed heart valves. Today rheumatic fever is easily cured with antibiotics. But back in 1937, when Dave was five years old, the disease was unstoppable and thousands of people died from it every year.

"I really don't remember her, what she looked like or how she treated me," he writes in his autobiography. "But I do remember when she was really sick and when she died."

Dave remembered the smell of the stark, white hospital room, the sheets, the nurses, and his mother's face. "The whole thing was like a strange dream to me," he recalls. "I didn't know people were supposed to die, and I didn't know who would replace her."

15

His grandma tried to comfort him, but she couldn't compensate for his father's rejection. "Minnie never liked my adoptive dad," Dave remembers. "He was working as an auto mechanic around the time my adoptive mother died and would complain about how bored he was with his job. My grandmother didn't want to hear his excuses." During the days surrounding his mother's death, Dave listened to his father and his grandmother fight. The discord must have made him feel that much more insecure.

His father, Rex Thomas, was a tall, loud man who worked in a variety of blue-collar mechanical jobs. He always had plenty of drinking buddies and married four times, so he was a distant father who never seemed interested in Dave. "I never remember him hugging me or showing any affection," Dave recalls.

Rex remarried about seven months after Auleva died. His new wife's name was Marie, and she worked full-time in a paper mill. She would come home exhausted at the end of the day and lash out at Dave. During meals Marie and Rex would ignore Dave except to criticize his table manners.

In less than three years Rex divorced Marie, and suddenly there was no woman in the house to cook their meals. So Dave and his dad began eating out. At the age of eight Dave Thomas discovered a new place that he loved: the world of restaurants. Everything about restaurants fascinated him. He loved the way each restaurant looked different and how their menus were decorated. He loved the way the food was presented on the plate and what the restaurant chose to offer as the daily specials.

But he found something even better than the food in restaurants. He loved to watch the people: families eating, talking, and laughing together. Dave observed them wistfully, seeing how happy other parents and children could be.

Even though Dave's dad didn't converse with his son during meals, Dave still treasured the times they shared together in the restaurants. "When we went out to eat, I

had my dad all to myself," he remembers. "Since he went out drinking with his friends a lot in the evenings, dinner was really the only time I had to spend with him."

Eating out so much gave Dave a perspective that would serve him well in his working career. By the age of nine he had become a real expert on restaurants. He knew what customers expected, and he knew what kind of service and quality were acceptable. He absorbed all the complaints and compliments he overheard and stored them away for future reference. Most of the time Dave and his father ate in neighborhood bars that featured hamburgers and hot dogs. Dave's favorite hamburger stand featured mouthwatering hamburgers with grilled onions and thick chocolate milk shakes.

The outbreak of World War II changed life for both

The beach and boardwalk of Atlantic City, where Dave Thomas was born in 1932. He never knew his birth mother; his adoptive mother, Auleva Thomas, died when Dave was five years old.

father and son. Many of Rex's friends were drafted, but Rex was too old for military service. He was contributing to the war effort by working in a factory in Evansville, Indiana. Because many younger men left their jobs to go into the army or navy, there was a shortage of workers for vital defense industry jobs, and women stepped in to fill the vacant positions. One such woman, named Viola, began dating Rex Thomas and soon became his third wife.

"Viola was a lot more attractive than Marie," Dave remembers. She was happy, and she was kind to Dave. She also had two daughters from a previous marriage, and for the first time there were other youngsters in the Thomas household. Betty was older than Dave, and Dona was younger.

In an interview for *Biography*, a TV program produced by the Arts and Entertainment Cable Network (A&E), Betty remembered what a strict man Rex was with his son. "David knew to mind him because he knew what kind of whippings he would get if he didn't," she said. "I don't think they were close, because I don't think anybody could have been really close to Rex. But he took care of David. He saw that he had clothes and food. But a loving man, a loving parent, he was not."

Both parents worked full-time. This gave Dave and Betty time to dream up some fun activities. They decided to try an unusual form of fund-raising: They dressed up like grown-ups and went around the neighborhood, knocking on people's doors to raise money for their church. "Since it was dark, nobody looked at us real close," Dave remembers. "And we really did give the money to the church." At the age of 10 Dave was already collecting money for good causes!

Even though Viola was much nicer to Dave than Rex's second wife, Marie, had been, according to Dave, she always saw to it that her daughters came first. "We had a small, little bedroom," stepsister Betty remembered in the A&E interview. "David slept on the couch. He didn't have a bedroom of his own."

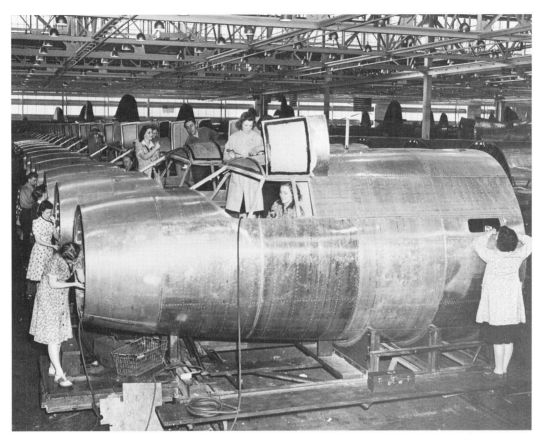

Life continued to be lonely for Dave. He describes himself as a "kid in between" because neither his father nor his stepmother ever seemed to notice or care about his need for love and attention. But Dave Thomas devised survival tactics that he used to get him through those rough times. He sought out people who would give him the love and attention he craved. And he always had a goal that he worked toward, one step at a time. But most of all he was always true to himself. He may have been quiet and shy, but he didn't try to be someone other than who he was.

Dave's first 10 years at home were almost devoid of happiness. But he always had someone who loved him very much. She lived many miles from his home, but from the age of five until he was nine years old, she taught Dave

With many young men serving in the military during World War II, factory jobs that were essential to the war effort were filled by women, such as these working on a bomber assembly line. Rex Thomas, who was too old for military service, met his third wife when they worked side by side in an Indiana factory.

When Dave visited his grand-mother Minnie Sinclair, he often spent time in the kitchen of Salstrum's Restaurant, where she worked.

what he now considers life's most important lessons. Her name was Minnie Sinclair, his maternal grandmother. Minnie was the strongest influence in Dave's young life.

"Minnie was a real strong-willed lady," Dave writes in his book. "She believed if you worked hard, you made things happen." Minnie had single-handedly raised her own four children to adulthood. Her husband had been killed in a railroad accident, and she had taken whatever work she could find to support her family.

For about four years after his mother died Dave spent his summer months with Minnie. Even though those summers were a relatively short amount of time in Dave's young life, her care filled some important needs for him.

Although she was old enough to be retired, Minnie was still working full-time when Dave came to visit. One of her jobs was to cook the dinner specials and wash the dishes at Salstrum's Restaurant near her home in Augusta, Michigan. Dave's memories of Salstrum's helped create his love of restaurants. He enjoyed the fast pace and high energy level necessary for food preparation. He loved watching the waiters and waitresses picking up and delivering orders.

But what lay beyond the kitchen intrigued him even more. As an employee Minnie used the back door of the restaurant to go to and from work. But one day Dave decided he wanted to see what the restaurant looked like through the front door. He went around and peered inside. It was as if he were looking into a grand palace, with row upon row of tables draped in white tablecloths. Even the silverware was engraved with a fancy monogrammed S.

"I had a good feeling there," he comments in his autobiography. "I would peek out front at the customers, who were eating, laughing, and having a good time. I could have stayed there all night just watching."

He liked the way the food was served, family style, in big bowls. All those families passing bountiful bowls of mashed potatoes, peas, chicken, and dumplings represented the very things Dave yearned for and did not have: a happy family, security, togetherness.

But on Saturdays Grandma Minnie did her best to make up for the rest of his lonely childhood. They would drive her Model-A Ford to town and spend the day at the five-and-dime. Dime stores were a smaller version of today's giant retail stores, like Kmart and Wal-Mart. They had many departments and sold everything from clothes and kitchen gadgets to parakeets and school supplies.

Dave liked everything about the five-and-dime store, including the large red sign on the front of the building. "To me that friendly sign stood for a good time," he remembers. "Maybe that's why I chose the color red for Wendy's store signs."

Minnie and Dave had a weekly ritual for their shopping trips to Kalamazoo, Michigan. Not too surprisingly, Dave and Minnie's routine included lunch at the store's lunch counter. He would choose one of the standard lunch counter sandwiches of the day—a sloppy joe, barbecue, or hot dog—with a frothy mug of root beer.

After lunch Dave would head for his favorite section of the store—the toy department. There he would browse through the toy pistols, cars, and trucks. Although Grandma Minnie didn't have much money, she often gave Dave enough to buy a small toy.

And he and Grandma Minnie never missed a visit to the candy counter. There bins of loose candy were measured out and sold by the pound. Dave and Minnie's favorite order was a half pound of candy orange slices and a half pound of bridge mix (a combination of caramels, raisins, and nuts, each coated with a hard chocolate shell).

Dave enjoyed the surprise of biting into a piece and discovering what was inside. "You never knew what you were biting into when you grabbed a piece—maybe a chocolate-covered raisin, a nut, cream center, or caramel," he recollects fondly.

Dave believes he learned some of life's most important lessons on those shopping trips with Minnie. She would feel the different bolts of cloth for sale and tell her grandson, "They're making this stuff thinner and thinner. They just don't put in the quality like when I was young. Quality is everything, David. Remember that. If people keep cutting corners, this country's going to be in big trouble."

Never cutting corners is a standard of quality that Dave has always remembered. Thirty-five years later, when a reporter asked Dave why Wendy's hamburger patties were square, Dave answered automatically, "At Wendy's we never cut corners."

Dave admired his grandmother for her ability to work hard while maintaining a clean, tidy house. "The white-painted exterior always looked fresh," he reminisces. "Inside, the house had linoleum floors and tabletops, and a big potbellied stove for heating . . . It was a simple house, but everything was kept neat as a pin."

Although Grandma Minnie never had much money, Dave was always impressed by the way she managed what she had. When he was younger, Dave used to dream that someday he would be wealthy so he could take his grandmother to the nicest store in town. He pictured himself encouraging her to pick out beautiful things of top quality.

Watching Minnie work hard also gave Dave a lifelong appreciation for women. He recognized that women in their forties and fifties had often helped their husbands, raised families, and put off their own desires; now many of them were ready to get going, to do something for themselves. "I have worked with a lot of women like this," Dave says in his book, "and they are fantastic. Men can't touch them in terms of drive, desire, and eagerness to work hard. I want these women to know that they're dynamite, and the business world needs them!"

Minnie also had a spiritual strength that, in turn, gave Dave the strength he needed to survive his lonely childhood. On a summer day when Dave was 11 years old, Grandma Minnie took him to a deep blue lake in Michigan. There he was baptized in the waters of Gull Lake.

For Minnie, Christianity meant more than doctrine. It meant working hard at her job in the restaurant, it meant caring for her lodgers, and it meant tending a big garden, doing the canning, and feeding the pigs every morning. "I got baptized into the roll-up-your-shirtsleeves kind of faith that Grandma Minnie held," said Dave years later. "And I believe in it to this day."

Other than those few precious summers in Michigan, Dave rarely saw his grandmother. But those days taught Dave the basic values of how he wanted to live when he grew up. And he used Minnie's love as a shield to protect himself from his adoptive father's withering criticism. No matter what his dad thought, Dave was determined to show Rex Thomas that he would be a success someday.

Dave Thomas was baptized a Christian in the waters of Gull Lake, Michigan.

Dave Thomas takes a short break to munch on one of his culinary creations. Dave's grandmother instilled in him a work ethic that he has maintained all his life.

3

WORK IT OUT

"WORK HARD, AND you won't feel so sorry for yourself." Dave learned this lesson for living from his grandma Minnie Sinclair, and he built his life on this rule. While other kids enjoyed the carefree days of childhood, Dave was looking for a way to get out of the house and earn some money.

Rex had moved Dave, his stepmother, and his two stepsisters to Princeton, Indiana, a small town in the southwestern part of the state. Although Dave was only 10, he took a job at a small gas station, watching over the gas pumps while the owner ate lunch. The station only had two pumps, so mostly Dave just hung around with little to do. "I don't even remember if he paid me," Dave said later, "but it was a place to go to get out of the house during the summers."

Dave took on another job, delivering newspapers. But with no one to help him understand the intricacies of folding the papers, finding the right addresses, and collecting the money, Dave soon gave up on the newspaper business. He went on to other unsatisfying jobs. Dave tried working as a golf caddie, then as a pinsetter in a bowling alley. Before the invention of the automatic pinsetter, bowling alleys would hire kids to set up the pins. "After one week in that noisy, dirty bowling alley, I thought it was a zero deal and quit," Dave remembers.

He dreamed that one day he could get a job in that most wonderful of professions—working in a restaurant. But no one would give a 10- or 11-year-old any kind of job working in a restaurant. But all that changed in the summer of 1944.

Rex Thomas had just moved the family again, this time to Knoxville, Tennessee. By now Dave had changed schools four times in six years. He never had a chance to make many friends, but he missed the ones he did make. That summer of 1944 he was dreading the struggle of trying to make new friends. He reacted by hanging around his house and sleeping in late. When Rex saw his son moping, he told Dave to go get a job. But what kind of job could a 12-year-old kid get?

One day on the main street of Knoxville, Dave saw a sign in a grocery store: Help Wanted. Dave went inside and told the owner—also named Dave—that he was 15. He was hired for 20 cents an hour and a sandwich at lunch. He worked from 8 A.M. to 4 P.M. sweeping the sidewalk in front of the store and delivering groceries on a bicycle.

In Knoxville delivering groceries was a difficult job. The terrain was steep, and riding a grocery-laden bike was a hard job. "When I got off the bike at the top of the hill and read the building mailboxes, one customer after another turned out to live on the fourth or fifth floor," he recalls. "After a couple weeks of that I had leg muscles like a mountain goat."

Even so, he stuck with it, dreaming about the money he was earning and how he would spend it. He longed for a new bike, and the thought of being able to buy one kept him pumping his bicycle up and down the Knoxville streets.

After one month the owner told Dave he was going on vacation for two weeks. That was just fine with Dave. The

summers in Knoxville were notoriously hot and humid, and Dave wanted to spend more time at the local swimming pool.

But a week later Dave's boss called and said he had cut his vacation short. Dave was disappointed. Hoping to postpone his return to work, he told his boss he had made some plans for the next week. When the Help Wanted sign went back into the grocery store's front window, Dave knew he had been fired. Dave says he learned a tough lesson that day: "When you take a job, you better be ready to show up for work when it suits your boss . . . not just when it suits you."

Undaunted, Dave applied for work at a drugstore in Knoxville the next week. Back in those days drugstores

When Dave Thomas was 12 years old, his father moved the family to Knoxville, Tennessee. It was in Knoxville that Dave got his first job, delivering groceries on his bicycle. To be hired, he had to tell the owner of the store that he was 15 years old.

Dave's job at the Regas Restaurant in Knoxville was a great learning experience. Dave worked there evenings, weekends, and summers for nearly two years, often with William Regas, the son of the owner, Frank Regas. (Today, William owns the restaurant.)

had soda fountains—counters with stools where people could sit down and enjoy an ice-cream sundae or soda. Dave yearned to work in some kind of food service. This time he told the manager he was 16; Dave got his wish, and he was hired to work the soda fountain, his first real restaurant job.

He had fun mixing sodas and making ice-cream floats and sundaes. He even enjoyed wearing the Walgreens uniform of white pants and a black bow tie. Standing behind that counter, taking orders, and making change made him feel special.

But after three weeks the manager began to suspect that Dave wasn't 16 after all. When Dave asked for some time off for a family obligation, the manager began asking questions, and Dave confessed his true age. The manager stopped scheduling him for work, and Dave lost the first job he ever loved.

Sad and disappointed, Dave Thomas told his father about losing his job at the drugstore. He thought his father would understand; after all, it wasn't Dave's fault he was only 12 years old. But Rex was not an understanding father. His father slammed his fist on the kitchen table and screamed, "You'll never keep a job! I'll be supporting you for the rest of your life!"

Dave promised himself that he would never lose another job again. This promise gave him the courage he needed to go back out and look for the right job. In downtown Knoxville he found that job.

The Regas Restaurant had a sign in its window that said the owners were hiring. Mustering up his courage, Dave went inside. He told the employee in charge of hiring that he wanted to work there because he loved the restaurant business. Dave also lied about his age again, claiming he was 16 years old.

"Little did brothers Frank and George Regas, owners of the Regas Restaurant, know, they had the youngest counterman in the state on their payroll," Dave remembers. "But I was in the restaurant business again. I was right where I wanted to be."

Surrounded by an atmosphere of friendly, working people, Dave found the acceptance and camaraderie he had never known at home. He loved his uniform—a gray smock with a white shirt and tie, and a starched white apron.

Dave became a coworker and friend of Frank's son Bill. Although Bill was four years older than Dave, they were both expected to work at a fast pace, and they did. The two were in charge of waiting on customers at the 17-stool counter. There Dave learned the waiter's art of carrying four plates of food and cups of coffee without using a tray and without spilling or dripping. He also learned how to take orders without writing them down. Even though as many as a hundred customers might be on his shift, Dave was required to memorize every order and then write out the check.

Work gave Dave's life a purpose, as well as a circle of friends that he had never had before. Dave worked every day during the summer and every weekend during the school year. He would begin work at 8 P.M. and work until 8 A.M. the next morning. The restaurant was open 24 hours a day, and workers from the nearby defense plants kept a steady stream of customers coming through the doors.

Dave's job covered many areas of the restaurant. He would wait on customers, and then at 2 A.M. he would help clean up the restaurant. When that was finished, he would make sandwiches for the next day's customers. Working with Gene Rankin, the Regases' brother-in-law, Dave would prepare as many as 400 egg, tuna, and ham sandwiches a night. Then he would work the breakfast shift from 4 to 8 A.M.

"This work style set a standard for me," he said later. "I became used to putting out a lot of volume when I was very young; I just thought that it was the way you were supposed to do it. If somebody pays you, it was up to you to perform."

Instead of resenting his long hours, Dave enjoyed learning the restaurant business while earning 25 cents an hour. That may sound like slave wages by today's standards, but back then a cup of coffee cost only a nickel. A meatloaf dinner with dessert cost 45 cents. So in the 1940s Dave was earning adult wages at the age of 12.

On Saturdays Dave would tell Gene about his secret desire to own his own restaurant. Although Gene was an adult, he took Dave's dream seriously. Dave was encouraged by Gene's attitude. But strangely, his father's attitude made him even more determined to achieve his goal.

He looked at his father's constant criticism as a challenge. According to Bill Regas, Dave said, "I'm gonna show my dad. I'm gonna get a job. I'm going to do well and make good money and I'm going to be successful."

But Rex didn't make it easy for Dave to succeed. About six months after Dave started working at the Regas, his father got a job 30 miles away in Oak Ridge. Rex knew how much Dave enjoyed working at the Regas Restaurant, so he gave Dave the option of riding a bus back and forth to his father's on the weekends. Dave jumped at the chance to stay with his restaurant "family."

When summer arrived again, Dave went to work full-time and rented a room near the Regas Restaurant for seven dollars a week. This allowed him to live on his own for the first time. For 13-year-old Dave Thomas this was a perfect situation. He was earning good money and making his own decisions.

Working for the Regas brothers gave Dave insight into the power of motivating an employee in a positive way. Every day one of the Regas brothers would tell him he was doing a good job. For someone who had never had many compliments in his life, this praise gave Dave the self-worth he needed to excel.

If he did make a mistake, the Regas brothers prefaced their discussion of the problem with a remark about the good work Dave was doing. "They never criticized me or made me feel small in front of anyone," Dave reminisces. "They made sure I'd learn from the mistakes without losing my drive, and still keep an upbeat attitude."

One evening Dave admitted to Gene that he had lied about his age. Instead of getting angry, Gene confessed that he and the rest of the people who worked there had suspected the truth from the beginning. "But you had such determination, we just decided to let it go," Gene told him.

When Dave was 14, Rex uprooted the family once again. This time, he moved the Thomas clan back to Indiana—too far from the Regas Restaurant for Dave to con-

In Fort Wayne, Dave answered an advertisement for a busboy at a restaurant called the Hobby House. This job would change his life.

tinue working there. Dave was sorry to leave the restaurant and all of the people who had become like family to him. "On my last day of work, Frank Regas took me aside and talked to me man to man," Dave recalls. He told Dave, "If you ever come back and want a job, it's yours."

Moving back to Indiana in 1947 was both good and bad for Dave. Rex had gotten a job in Fort Wayne, a town just 100 miles from Minnie Sinclair's Michigan home. But the bad part was *really* bad: Rex moved his family into a house trailer with no indoor toilet. A new baby in the family further complicated the already cramped living conditions.

"It was really rough going back to living with the family every day," Dave admits. "I had had a taste of independence in Knoxville, and I wanted it again." So Dave tried the one remedy he knew best. He went looking for a job in a restaurant.

This time he found an advertisement in the newspaper

for a new short-order coffeehouse just opening up in Fort Wayne. The Hobby House Restaurant needed a busboy. Dave needed a way back into the restaurant business. It was a connection that would have historic significance throughout Dave's life.

When Dave Thomas was still in high school, he refused to move away from Fort Wayne with his father. Instead, the 15-year-old stayed at the local YMCA and worked full-time at the Hobby House while attending school. "What I did is not something I'd recommend to any kid today," Dave later wrote in his autobiography Well Done!

4

FROM THE HOBBY HOUSE TO THE MESS HALL

FOR HIS INTERVIEW at the Hobby House Restaurant, Dave dressed up in his nicest clothes. He had already learned how to make a good first impression from his days with the Regas family.

During the interview Dave promised the manager that he would be the best busboy the Hobby House ever employed. Dave was hired on the spot because, the manager told him, he liked Dave's attitude.

After the interview Dave noticed a man wearing a suit who was sweeping floors and clearing tables. Later Dave learned that the man in the suit was Phil Clauss, owner of the Hobby House. Phil's son Richard remembers the way Dave's work ethic impressed his father. "My dad got a kick out of it, a young man with that kind of attitude," Richard recalled in an A&E television interview. "Instead of asking, 'How much do I make?' and 'What time do I get off?' here was a kid who really wanted to learn and really work for him."

Dave was hired for 50 cents an hour; after a week he got a raise to 55 cents an hour. His first goal was to work hard and be promoted to the soda fountain job, the same job he had enjoyed years earlier in the

35

drugstore. After four weeks Dave got his wish for the fountain job, and he began scooping up sundaes, banana splits, and milk shakes.

Dave's enthusiasm sent him up the promotional ladder at the Hobby House. After a month on the fountain job Dave was promoted to the kitchen staff, and his pay was raised to $35 for a 50-hour work week.

"The hard work was paying off," Dave says. "I felt good about myself and about my work, and I was feeling real close to the other people who worked there. They were becoming like a family to me."

When Rex Thomas announced that he was moving the family again at the end of the summer, Dave announced that he was staying in Fort Wayne. Dave didn't ask his father if he could stay in Fort Wayne, and Rex didn't argue with him or try to change his mind. In fact, Rex didn't seem at all surprised.

In an unusually emotional moment, Dave began crying and told his father, "Someday you'll be proud of me. I'm going to have my own restaurant, and I'm going to be a success."

"I hope you're right, son," his dad replied. "Good luck to you."

And with that brief reply Rex and his family were gone from Dave's life. Other than Christmas cards and the occasional phone call, that was the end of Dave's emotionally barren relationship with Rex.

In many of the country's larger cities, young men who couldn't afford to rent apartments could rent a room at the local Young Men's Christian Association, or YMCA. Dave rented a room at the "Y" because it was only a block away from work and an easy walk to the high school. "What I did is not something I'd recommend to any kid today," Dave said years later. "I was fifteen years old, working fifty hours a week minimum, still in Fort Wayne Central High School, and living at the Y."

In the 10th grade Dave wrote an essay entitled "The Pur-

Phil Clauss, the owner of the Hobby House, took young Dave Thomas under his wing.

suit Of Happiness." In the essay Dave explained that enjoy-
ing your work is the most important aspect of working:

> Do the work you like to do. You maybe could earn more
> money by being the president of the company, but would
> you be happy? You would be better off being a truck dri-
> ver than you would being the president of the company if
> you like driving trucks best.

Dave also laid out his vision of what he wanted in life
and how he would go about getting it:

When the pressure of juggling work and school became too much, Dave dropped out of Fort Wayne Central High School after 10th grade—a decision he later regretted.

Before I ever go into business for myself, I am going to know my business. I am going to start on a small scale and build my business and my experience together. After I finish school, I want to join the army for a while and be a cook. In this way, I will be getting more experience. I will have my education and my army experience. I will be all set to start the pursuit of happiness with a restaurant of my own.

Dave's essay was published in the school's newspaper, the *Spotlight*. Although Dave wasn't an aspiring writer, his teacher saved his essay, and in later years she read it to her classes. It was a prophetic piece of writing, but that wasn't the only reason she saved it. She saved it because she was impressed that a 10th-grade student would have such a clear idea of what he wanted to do with his life.

Unfortunately, Dave had such focus that he decided he did not need a high-school education. He dropped out of school in 1947, after finishing 10th grade. He wanted to learn the restaurant business; this was something that wasn't taught at Fort Wayne Central High, and the teenager felt that he could learn more by working full-time. Many years later, Dave Thomas would describe his decision to leave high school early as "the biggest mistake of my life."

Dave's busy work schedule did not provide many social opportunities, something most 15-year-old boys need and want. He might have spent all of his spare time hanging around the YMCA, but for Phil Clauss. The restaurant owner liked Dave and kept an eye on him. When Clauss noticed that Dave seemed lonely, he suggested that Dave rent a room from his sister and her husband, Lloyd and Esther Marquart. Dave's decision to move out of the YMCA turned out to be a good one. "They were wonderful people, and some of my happiest times were spent with them," Dave remembers. "I gave them a token amount of money for rent, and they gave me something money can't buy—a sense of belonging."

The Marquarts felt the same about their young tennant. "Dave was like our oldest son," Esther Marquart told A&E's *Biography*.

Having a family to live with and a job with plenty of room for promotion was working out well for Dave. But when the Korean War started, Dave knew he wanted to enlist in the military. After all, training as an Army cook was one of the steps in Dave's strategic plan for his success.

Although Dave was only 17 years old, Rex gave his legal permission for his son to join the army. In 1950, just after his 18th birthday, Dave reported for basic training at Fort Benning, Georgia.

Dave was no sooner in basic training than he developed an infected tooth. He needed a root canal and was taken out of basic training for 10 days until his swollen, sore jaw returned to normal. To stave off the boredom, Dave moseyed down to the mess hall and volunteered to do light work such as sweeping floors and clearing tables.

Once again Dave's basic initiative paid off. Some of the cooks were problem drinkers who wouldn't show up for work. When the mess hall sergeant asked Dave if he would like to enroll in the army's Cook and Baker's School, Dave leaped at the chance. While other GIs were marching with 50-pound field packs and crawling under barbed-wire obstacle courses, Dave was learning the finer points of cake baking.

Not that the Cook and Baker's School was a tea party. The eight-week program was a crash course in measuring and baking in large quantities. Students worked a 24-hour shift preparing breakfast, lunch, and dinner before taking a 24-hour break.

In spite of Dave's work ethic, the baking side of the school began to overwhelm him. "You had to know how to use the ovens," Dave explains. "I didn't know how to use them. It was called 'cake disaster.' I had about 40 sheet pans of cakes that were strictly raw in the middle. I mean, it was a nightmare." But as he always had, Dave worked hard to learn what he needed to succeed.

When Dave finished his training at the Cook and Baker School, he was assigned to an army division that would be sent either to Germany, which was still being occupied by U.S. troops in the aftermath of World War II, or to Korea, where a war had begun. Most GIs were hoping they could go to Germany. A few peaceful years of service there were vastly preferable to taking part in a conflict in which more than 2.7 million people eventually were killed, including over 54,000 American soldiers.

Dave was pleased when he learned he would be going to Germany, and surprised when he was promoted to the rank of sergeant. His hard work and willingness to do whatever was asked of him had won him his first army promotion.

"Did volunteering get me there?" Dave asked himself many years later. "Partly. When a division shipped out overseas, every slot on the table of the organization had to be filled. They needed just so many captains, corporals

and so on. There was a vacancy for a sergeant, which I hadn't even known about. A little initiative will improve your luck nine days out of ten."

In an operation as large and complex as the military, distribution problems are bound to occur. So when Dave arrived in Germany, he used his bartering skills to trade with other units for things he needed. Dave's commanding officer gave him permission to use the general's jeep to go out and trade.

"I was slowly making a name for myself," Dave says. "The company commander, mess officer, and mess sergeant really liked what I was doing. They made me their underground, unofficial procurement officer. Their permission and their vote of confidence were all that I needed."

Dave's biggest achievement as a mess sergeant had almost nothing to do with food—but it had everything to do with morale. Dave noticed that the men complained

When the Korean War started, Dave decided to join the U.S. Army. In the military he continued preparing for a restaurant career, receiving training at the army's eight-week Cook and Baker's School. There, army cooks like the one pictured here learned how to prepare good meals for large numbers of soldiers.

about the dingy walls in the mess hall. He realized how important it was to serve food in pleasant surroundings. But all of his attempts to find paint for the mess hall were thwarted. Every official refusal only made Dave more determined to succeed. He filed requests everywhere he could think of to file them.

One day Dave finally received a shipment of 500 gallons of paint. It was his proudest achievement. "When I presented the paint to my mess hall sergeant, my reputation turned to gold," Dave recalls. "Each company was evaluated on appearance, and after we painted the mess hall and the barracks, we got a high rating. Most important, the troops were proud. You could tell by the way they walked and joked when they came in for chow."

For most army cooks, giving the mess hall a new look would have been more than enough of an achievement. But Dave had more challenges to pursue. A new opportunity presented itself to him during a conversation with his roommate, Master Sergeant Ed McCauley.

McCauley managed the Enlisted Men's Club. The club served food, even though it was more of a bar than a restaurant. When Dave started suggesting new items for the menu to boost food sales, McCauley tried them and was pleased with the results. When McCauley asked Dave if he wanted to be the assistant manager of the club, Dave was ready. Not only was it a considerable boost in pay, but it was also a job that was usually reserved for career soldiers with 20 years of service.

"Working at the Club was my first opportunity to build and turn around a restaurant operation that was flat on its back," Dave explains. "And because it was a government facility and didn't have any shareholders, I was able to take risks without having to mortgage my house or be afraid I'd lose my job overnight."

Instead of trying to turn the club into a fancy restaurant, Dave focused on changing the menu from cold sandwiches to warm snacks that were popular back home.

He introduced chicken in a basket, hamburgers, meat loaf, steak sandwiches, and hot roast beef sandwiches. He even added shrimp cocktail. Dave's menu caught on with the enlisted men, and food sales skyrocketed from $40 to $700 a day.

But success stories often come with some tough lessons. Dave learned that being the boss is not as easy as it looks. The Enlisted Men's Club employed about 15 German civilians. These people were good workers when Dave's boss was around, but the minute he left, they ignored Dave.

Dave had two problems: First, under a postwar United Nations agreement, the army had to go through the German government to fire any civilians from their jobs. Second, the Germans traditionally did not promote young people to positions of authority. Dave was only 19, and the Germans resented taking orders from someone much younger than them.

But Dave was determined to make his job work without going to his boss. So he called a meeting and got an interpreter to translate his words into German. "I am your boss, and the way you have been treating me is not right," Dave told them. He went on to say that if they did not start accepting him and doing what he said, he would fire each one of them. If they wanted to work for him and do a good job, fine. If not, Dave told them, they could hit the road and never come back.

Dave ended his speech by asking if everyone understood. He looked each person in the eye—and not one person left. Dave had shown that he was in command. What's more, he had learned a valuable lesson at the age of 19.

While other soldiers were using their free time to see other parts of Europe, Dave worked every night at the club except his night off. He spent the entire two and a half years of duty hard at work.

When he was discharged from the army, Dave decided he would go home and pick up where he had left off at the

Dave serves a hamburger to a Wendy's customer in a store built on the site of the Hobby House Restaurant in Fort Wayne. After leaving the army, Dave returned to the Hobby House to work.

Hobby House Restaurant. He also went to visit Grandma Minnie. She gave him more information about his birth family. He learned from Grandma Minnie that his birth mother, Mollie, had lived around Philadelphia, so he went there to try to find her.

Back then there were no organizations that helped adopted kids find information about their birth parents. Dave didn't know where to start, so he went to the police station. One of the officers read Dave's adoption papers and some letters that Mollie had written to Minnie. From this he determined that Dave's mother had lived in Camden, New Jersey.

Dave's birth grandparents still lived at the address in Camden. His grandfather was a tailor, and Dave saw his sewing machines and bolts of thread. His grandmother was very sick but still living. They told him that his mother had died about two years before from rheumatic fever, just like his adoptive mother. He learned that Mollie had worked in a restaurant for a while as a waitress. She married a man named Joe and never had any other children.

No one mentioned his birth father, however, and he got the impression that they didn't want to talk about him. So Dave resigned himself to the possibility that he might never know who his birth father was.

Meanwhile, a whole new set of challenges waited for Dave. When he returned to the Hobby House Restaurant in Fort Wayne, Dave Thomas met the person who would help him create the family he had always wanted.

Within 15 years after leaving the army, Dave had made himself a millionaire, thanks to his success in promoting Kentucky Fried Chicken and managing a string of restaurants.

5

LEAVING THE ARMY, MEETING THE COLONEL

AFTER HIS STINT in the army Dave returned to the Hobby House Restaurant in Fort Wayne. His boss, Phil Clauss, gave him an official welcome home. "My first day back was a real special homecoming for me," he says. "The whole bunch was there, including Phil Clauss, who met me at the door holding my old apron."

But things would never be the same at the Hobby House. A new waitress named Lorraine Buskirk had been hired while Dave was away. She was petite, but she had a strong voice and a positive outlook. Even though she was just 18, Dave noticed her strength.

Lorraine remembers they were attracted to each other even though sparks occasionally flew between them at work. "He was a short-order cook and I was a waitress," she told A&E's *Biography*. "We used to fight because he used to try to tell me how to be a waitress and I told him he had to learn to be a cook."

Dave's version of their stormy beginnings, recounted in *Dave's Way*, differs only slightly:

One day we were really busy, and I kept pushing the orders out onto the counter at top speed, ringing the bell when an order was ready so the waitresses knew their food was up. Lorraine wasn't picking up her orders fast enough to suit me, so I just stood there ringing the bell over and over. After about 10 rings she stormed up to me holding two plates in her hands. "Listen," she said, "would you like me to serve this food, or do you want to wear it?"

The Hobby House staff worked late, and usually the crew didn't finish with clean-up duties until around 1 A.M. Dave would always give the waitresses a ride home. "I started being the last one on the list that he would drop off," Lorraine recalls. "We used to go out for a sandwich or coffee or something after work and just talk and get to know each other."

Lorraine's parents liked Dave, and in 1954 Dave and Lorraine were married. The wedding guests consisted of the staff from the Hobby House and some of Lorraine's friends. The wedding party included the bride, the groom, and Esther and Lloyd Marquart, Phil Clauss's sister and brother-in-law, who had given Dave a home and family after Rex left Fort Wayne.

The Hobby House waitresses predicted that Dave's marriage to Lorraine would never last. Today, more than 45 years later, the Thomases are proud to say that those waitresses' predictions were wrong.

Dave and Lorraine bought a small house with a $7,500 loan from Hobby House owner Phil Clauss. Soon after that, in January of 1955, their first daughter, Pam, was born. Now Dave had the family he had always wanted. But his goals didn't allow for time at home with the family. "I left the responsibility of the house and the child to Lorraine," he says. "I had no real idea of what a father should be like. How strict should he be? Should he spank his kids? How much should he give in to them? How many things like money and gifts should be given them? Lorraine made the decisions; I was no model father who shared in taking care of the home."

On A&E's *Biography*, Pam Thomas described her dad

The first Kentucky Fried Chicken restaurant, owned by Colonel Harland Sanders, was located in Corbin, Kentucky. Today, this building is the Sanders Cafe and Museum.

during her early childhood. "I remember living in Fort Wayne and my dad working at the Hobby House and my dad coming home with these black shoes that were just [covered with] grease because he worked as a cook," she said. "I remember going there for dinner because my dad would be there and that's the only time we ever saw him."

Working was what Dave knew best. His workday lasted from 12 to 14 hours; he earned $75 a week. In 1956, Phil Clauss opened a new restaurant, called the Ranch House, and put Dave in charge. The Ranch House featured barbecued ribs. Although the food was good, the menu had too many choices, and the cooks couldn't focus on any one specialty. But all that lack of focus would change after Dave learned about a Kentucky colonel who had a new way to sell chicken.

Colonel Harland Sanders helped create the fast-food business by accident. When his own restaurant was bypassed by the newly built interstate highway that ran by Corbin, Kentucky, the Colonel looked for a new way to sell

Colonel Sanders helped to create the fast-food business by franchising his method of cooking chicken to other restaurants. Phil Clauss and Dave Thomas were among the first to sell the Colonel's Kentucky Fried Chicken.

his chicken recipe. The Colonel came up with a new idea: if restaurant owners bought the Colonel's secret recipe and the pressure cookers necessary to prepare the chicken correctly, they would be granted the right to sell his "Kentucky Fried Chicken." The Colonel would be paid a nickel for every chicken sold.

At first Dave was completely unimpressed. "Why should we pay this guy a nickel a head when we already have good fried chicken ourselves?" Dave asked Phil Clauss.

Phil had a good answer. The method most restaurants used to make fried chicken was time-consuming. The chicken had to be cleaned, breaded, and then fried in grease in heavy cast-iron skillets. After the frying stage the chicken was put into Dutch ovens to cook the rest of the way. It was messy, and it took four hours to prepare the chicken. But the Colonel's cooking method used a deep-fry pressure cooker that reduced the cooking time to 30 minutes. With his method, chicken could be made every day, throughout the day as needed.

One day the Colonel showed up at the restaurant where Dave was working as an assistant manager. The Colonel would have been hard to miss. Sporting snow-white hair and a matching goatee, Harland Sanders looked the part of a Kentucky colonel right down to his gold-headed cane. The Colonel sat down, ordered a plate of ribs, and ate in silence. When he had finished, he paid the check and asked to see Dave.

"We sat down over a cup of coffee, and he talked to me

like an old friend," Dave recalls. "I've never met a better salesman. When he left, I had a sense this man was going to change my life." But it was going to take a super salesman to convince Dave that he had any interest in chicken. The truth was, Dave hated everything about chicken.

His hatred started back when Dave was 14 years old. His family was living in Tennessee, and Rex was working as a superintendent in a bus company. Rex and Dave had been invited for Sunday dinner by one of Rex's workers. Even as a poor kid Dave was shocked when they arrived at the worker's broken-down, dirty house.

"When we sat down to eat, some chickens started walking through the house," Dave remembers. "When they passed by my chair, the smell and the flies they drew turned my stomach. I couldn't stand it and had to go to the car. That was it. The end of me and chicken."

Or so he thought. When he finally tasted the Colonel's chicken, Dave was sold. He needed three months to install the equipment and teach the cooking staff how to prepare the chicken and the crackling gravy just right. "You wouldn't believe how particular he was about his crackling gravy," Dave says. "Cracklings are bits of fried flour that flake off the chicken after it's cooked, and you had to add enough cracklings to the gravy or the Colonel would really get after you."

Lorraine remembers that the Colonel "was a funny man. He used to cuss like a stevedore [a person who works on a dock unloading ships]. He had a temper, but he was always nice to me. He was kind of a strange man. He used to take his wife and his ex-wife to the conventions. Now, how about *them* apples?"

From the first day, Kentucky Fried Chicken was a success at the Ranch House restaurant. "We were on the edge of a new phenomenon and we were smart enough to see it," Dave says. So Phil and Dave built one of the first carry-out chicken stores in the United States. Way back in the 1950s the store was selling $3,000 to $4,000 worth of chicken every Sunday.

That would have been the end of the story for most restaurant owners. But Phil and Dave both wanted to see how much chicken they could sell if they really promoted their product. At the time most restaurants didn't advertise very much. If a restaurant became popular, it was because customers told friends, so the reputation spread by word of mouth.

But Phil and Dave had bigger dreams than that for their restaurant empire. So they kept inventing ways to make Kentucky Fried Chicken a household name. One day Dave called the Colonel and asked him if they could paint a picture of the Colonel's face on Dave's white Thunderbird convertible.

"Oh, that would be too ostentatious," the Colonel replied. Then the Colonel thought for a moment and asked Dave, "When can we get that done?"

Phil came up with the idea of using a paper bucket in which to sell the fried chicken. It made sense because a bucket could hold more than a flimsy paper box or bag. Phil's brother-in-law, Jim Chamberlain, had a local advertising agency, so they hired Jim to do sketches of Colonel Sanders for the bucket designs. This was the first time fast food had a face and a personality. Soon everyone wanted "the Colonel's chicken."

Colonel Sanders began appearing on local TV and radio programs, proclaiming his secret recipe of herbs and spices, and talking about the quality of his chicken. Dave would bring the Colonel to a radio station along with a bucket or two of free chicken. The Colonel became a familiar sight and a welcome guest on many shows.

Dave Thomas had relied on several mentors to teach him the restaurant business. However, it was a visitor who came to check out his Kentucky Fried Chicken triumph that eventually became Dave's ultimate role model for success.

Kenny King owned a group of restaurants in Cleveland in the late 1950s. When Kenny came to the Hobby House

Dave Thomas became a restaurant owner in 1962 when he turned around four failing Kentucky Fried Chicken restaurants in Columbus, Ohio. Phil Clauss, who owned the restaurants, promised to make Dave a partner if he would manage the money-losing stores.

to investigate the Kentucky Fried Chicken operation, Dave explained why it was such a popular product. Even though Dave was only the assistant manager of one restaurant, Kenny invited him to Cleveland to see his operation of 20 restaurants. "Here I was, twenty-five years old, making less than $100 a week, talking like an equal to someone who was making over $100,000 a year," Dave recalled.

Kenny eventually became one the Colonel's more successful franchisees (a person granted the right to sell another company's goods) of Kentucky Fried Chicken. And Dave saw in Kenny the kind of successful business-man he would like to be.

Kenny generously shared his ideas about business and personal goals with Dave. Kenny's philosophy for success boiled down to three basics: Follow the Ten Commandments, be honest with yourself, and support your family.

Dave never forgot Kenny's help and guidance. When Dave and Lorraine had a baby boy, they named him Kenny in his honor.

In 1962 Phil Clauss desperately needed Dave's help. Phil owned four Kentucky Fried Chicken restaurants in Columbus, Ohio, and they were in danger of going broke. Clauss owned the restaurants, but he was willing to give Dave a piece of the ownership if he would move to Columbus and take over their management.

Phil's offer was everything Dave had been waiting for. He has said that when the time is right to make a move, a person will just know it—"Deep down the green light clicks on." Well, Dave's green light was flashing. He knew he was ready. Lorraine and he talked it over, and they decided they could handle the risks involved. After all, at that time, they didn't have all that much to lose.

So in June of 1962 Dave and Lorraine moved to the Columbus suburb of Westerville. Dave plunged all of his energy into saving the restaurants. Meanwhile, even the Colonel thought he was crazy to take on the ailing restaurants. "I'm telling you for the last time, Dave" the Colonel said. "As your friend, get out now while you can. Things are just too far gone here. Listen to the Colonel, boy."

But nothing would stop Dave from achieving his goal. First he fired all four managers of the stores. Then he used the tactic that had gotten him promoted in the army: Dave bought paint and gave all the stores a fresh, clean coat. In order to find out exactly how much money the stores were making, Dave next devised a daily report sheet to keep track of expenses, sales, and cash in the bank. The form

was such a great record-keeping device that eventually the Colonel made copies of Dave's daily report sheet and used them in all of his restaurants.

Borrowing another successful tactic he'd used in the past, Dave began to promote and advertise his four restaurants. When one radio station manager offered to give Dave some radio advertising in exchange for chicken, a lightbulb went on in Dave's head. "It dawned on me that it wasn't our menu that was drawing people in. It was our chicken!"

Immediately Dave started thinking about all the unnecessary items on the menu. He cut out all the extra food that made the menu too long, keeping only the chicken, salads, dessert, and beverages. And then he promoted the daylights out of his chicken, printing coupons and running specials.

All of Dave's profits went back into a major advertising

Dave shows a Wendy's employee how he wants food to be prepared. Dave has always insisted that his employees not cut corners. "If the product wasn't right, he would grab the tray and throw it right in the garbage and tell the manager, 'Start all over and do it right. If you can't do it right, don't do it at all,'" his son Ken has commented.

effort. He found a sign maker in Columbus to build a large, revolving bucket painted like a Kentucky Fried Chicken container. The Colonel was soon using the spinning bucket signs for all of his stores, too.

Dave was slowly turning the restaurants into profitable stores. But he worked hard and nonstop to make it happen. "He wasn't doing much of anything except going to the stores and working—and it was work," Lorraine remembers. "Back then it wasn't just mental, it was physical labor. He was cooking, and he would come home at night smelling like fried chicken and grease."

His son, Ken, remembers days when his dad would lose patience when he found poorly prepared chicken being sold at his stores: "He would go to a KFC store and if the product wasn't right, he would grab the tray and throw it right in the garbage and tell the manager, 'Start all over and do it right. If you can't do it right, don't do it at all.'"

Dave's relentless work schedule and advertising efforts began to pay off, though. He not only saved the four restaurants from going under, but he also turned them into dynamic money-making operations. By March of 1967 Dave was able to pay back the $250,000 Phil had loaned to him in exchange for 40 percent ownership of the four restaurants. Dave opened a fifth restaurant—and that was successful, too.

When he talked to A&E, John Niklas remembered Dave's determination to own the top-selling chicken restaurant in Columbus. "He really didn't want anyone else to be selling chicken in Columbus, Ohio, other than Kentucky Fried Chicken," John said. "There were probably two other competitors at the time, and I remember Dave being absolutely ecstatic when one of them went out of business in this town. And to see boards on their windows, Dave said he had been successful."

In 1968 Dave and Phil sold their stores to the Kentucky Fried Chicken Corporation for $1.5 million. Dave's share of the business, along with stock he received in KFC Corporation totaled $1 million. At the age of 35, Dave was a millionaire. "The turnaround of Kentucky Fried Chicken in Columbus was the big breakthrough for me," Dave says "It made everything else possible in my career."

Having all that money was a wonderful feeling—but more important, he had proved that he was able to do what he'd set out to do from the beginning. The Thomas family was financially secure now. They didn't have to worry about how to pay the bills anymore—and all that money in the bank took the sting out of what Dave's dad had said about him so many years ago. Dave had demonstrated that he could certainly hold a job.

Dave and Lorraine celebrated their good fortune by going out to dinner—and not for fried chicken! But even though they now had financial security, the Thomas family continued to live a modest lifestyle. Lorraine did reward the kids by having a swimming pool built in their backyard. To remind everyone where the money came from to pay for it, she had the pool built in the shape of a chicken.

One of Dave's regrets, however, is that his friendship with the Colonel did not survive the success of Kentucky Fried Chicken. Colonel Sanders sold his business in order to retire, but he was not the type of person who could be happy in retirement. One day the Colonel blew up at Dave and never spoke to him again. "We saw each other maybe once or twice after that before he died at the age of ninety, but the relationship was history," Dave says. "To this day, I really admire him and like him, even though he was a tough customer to get along with sometimes."

When he ran the KFC restaurants, Dave even wore black string ties, just like the Colonel did—until people started asking him if he played with a country/western band.

Today, it is common to see a strip of chain restaurants, like Wendy's and the other stores pictured here, along busy highways.

6

HAMBURGER HYSTERIA AND THE BIRTH OF WENDY'S

"I THOUGHT MY big deal in life had been Kentucky Fried Chicken," Dave reflected during his A&E *Biography* interview. "I thought that I was never going to strike anything that big again. But I was wrong."

After 25 years of hard work, when Dave sold his share in the restaurants to the Kentucky Fried Chicken Corporation in 1968, he could afford to cut back on his work hours and enjoy his success. But that wasn't how Dave became a millionaire, and he certainly wasn't about to start taking it easy now.

His daughter Pam describes him as a man who did not know how to play. "He did not know how to enjoy life like a lot of people do with their family going to the beach," she said. "He did not know how to do that kind of stuff. He knew how to work, and work was where he got his kudos."

So what does a workaholic do after he becomes a millionaire?

"I still had it in my head to open my own restaurant, and I was more convinced than ever that it would be a place selling hamburgers," Dave says in his autobiography. "But I wasn't ready to make the move yet."

Fast-food hamburger restaurants have their roots in lunch carts of the 19th and early 20th centuries. These lunch carts still exist today, such as the one Dale Shaffer has operated in downtown Columbus, Ohio, for more than 20 years.

In the meantime, the two men who had taken over Kentucky Fried Chicken from Colonel Sanders and bought Dave and Phil's stores offered Dave a job. He would be regional head of operations for all the KFC stores east of the Mississippi River. Dave still wanted a steady paycheck, and he certainly knew the KFC food operation backward and forward, so he took the job.

But working for someone else was no longer challenging or interesting. And when Dave discovered that the new owners had misrepresented a legal problem in order to take advantage of him, he quit on the spot.

After seven months of working for someone else, Dave was out of a job. "Like my adoptive dad predicted, I was out of work, and I was only thirty-seven," he comments in *Dave's Way*. "The only difference was that I had several million in the bank and a gold mine of an idea in my head."

But Dave was nervous about following through on that idea, even though he thought his plan for a hamburger restaurant would be a winner, and even though he had proven that his philosophy of hard work would make him successful. The thought of being without a steady paycheck was unsettling. "When you've been poor, you always have that fear that you might be poor again, and you lie awake worrying at night," Dave says. "I was scared."

He got a job offer from a national fast-food chain of fish-and-chips restaurants called Arthur Treacher's. Although this wasn't his dream job, he took it. The problem was, though, Dave liked fish even less than he liked chicken. And the yearning to create a hamburger restaurant was the only idea that truly excited him.

By the late 1960s, hamburgers had become one of the most popular foods in the United States and around the world. In the book *Hamburger Heaven*, author Jeffrey Tennyson traced the origin of the hamburger in America to the late 1800s, when people began eating burgers for the same reason people eat them today: they were in a big hurry.

In the large American industrial cities of the East and Midwest, workers needed an inexpensive, quick way to eat lunch. Going home to eat took too long. So lunch counters and street vendors began selling hot food that could be eaten on the run. In 1856, the newspaper *Harper's Weekly* described the eating habits of this busy group of workers: "They swallow, but they don't eat; and like a boa constrictor, they bolt everything."

By 1872 hamburgers were being sold from horse-drawn wagons that would stop near the gates of factories. At that time the going rate was two hamburgers for a nickel. Eventually the wagons were replaced by dining cars with seats. When the dining cars lost their wheels and stayed in one spot, they became diners.

Another early haven for hamburgers was the soda fountain. During the Civil War, drugstores began installing counters where they sold soda water mixed with flavored

Drug store soda fountains were popular spots to get a soda and a quick meal.

syrup. These beverages were the first carbonated soft drinks. When one soda fountain in Philadelphia ran out of syrup, a counterman used ice cream instead and created ice-cream sodas. By 1908 there were approximately 75,000 soda fountains in the United States. It wasn't long before the fountains added quick meals of hamburgers, soups, and sandwiches.

Not to be outdone, dime stores throughout America installed luncheonette counters to provide a quick, hot meal to customers. In cities the "greasy spoon" lunch counters served food 24 hours a day. Hamburgers were a favorite item on their menus.

Even though no one can determine for sure who really invented the modern version of the hamburger, in *Ham-*

burger Heaven Jeffrey Tennyson wrote that are four serious contenders for that title.

In 1900 Louis Lassen owned a lunch counter in New Haven, Connecticut, that is still in business today. One day Lassen took steak trimmings, molded them into a patty, cooked it, and served it between two slices of bread. The hamburgers at Louis's Lunch are still made today, by Lassen's grandson Ken, using the same ingredients.

A second hamburger creation story has it that Charlie Nagreen of Seymour, Wisconsin, invented the burger in 1885 when he was only 15 years old. Nagreen had a concession wagon at the Outgamie County Fair, and he was doing a good business. But people wanted to stroll through the exhibits and eat, so Nagreen put beef between bread slices and named it the hamburger.

The third version of this American success story credits Frank Menches of Akron, Ohio. Menches was working a county fair concession booth in 1892 when he ran low on meat. In an effort to stretch his supplies, Menches ground it into sausage and made it into a patty. When Menches died in 1951 at the age of 86, the *Los Angeles Daily News* obituary headline proclaimed, "Hamburger Inventor Dies."

The fourth hamburger inventor is Fletcher Davis, who created his sandwich at his lunch counter in Athens, Texas. When the 1904 World's Fair opened in St. Louis, a reporter for the *New York Tribune* noticed the hamburger was "an innovation of a food vendor on the pike [midway]." Modern research—and Fletcher's relatives—suggest that this vendor was Fletcher Davis.

Whoever invented it, the hamburger was a food that people wanted. Before long, hamburgers and chain restaurants found each other. In 1916 two hamburger enthusiasts by the names of Walt Anderson and Billy Ingram founded White Castle Hamburgers. Anderson is given credit for inventing one of the major hamburger innovations: the bun. Anderson tested out his new product—a flattened patty infused with chopped onions—when he was still a short-order cook working for someone else.

The response was so enthusiastic that Anderson convert-ed a trolley car into a five-stool diner and started cranking out his version of the hamburger. He also came up with a griddle big enough to grill dozens of hamburgers at a time.

When the team opened its fourth restaurant, the build-ing was made of concrete blocks that were designed to look like stone. The roof had a turret and castle motif. At Ingram's suggestion, they painted the building white to give it a clean look and called it White Castle Hamburgers.

Today White Castle is still a popular hamburger chain with a loyal following. A slew of imitators sprang up, with names such as White Tower, White Huts, White Mannas, White Domes, and even White Midgets.

Life in the fast lane created more business opportunities. By 1920, 9 million Americans owned automobiles. A year later, restaurateur J. O. Kirby said, "People with cars are so lazy that they don't want to get out of them to eat." Kirby went on to prove his theory of human nature by founding America's first drive-in, the Pig Stand, in Dallas, Texas. The Pig Stand sold both barbecue and hamburgers, and by the mid-1930s there were 30 Pig Stands across the country.

From the 1930s until the 1950s, drive-ins were designed as futuristic restaurants, but the menu stuck to the favorites—hamburgers, french fries, carbonated bever-ages, and shakes. But many more innovations were on the way. Bob Wian invented the "Big Boy" by cutting a sesame-seed bun into three layers and adding two burgers, lettuce, cheese, and relish. Soon he had named his sand-wich, and he, too, spawned a series of imitators.

Maurice and Richard McDonald sold hamburgers for 35 cents apiece at their successful drive-in restaurant in San Bernardino, California. But they grew bored with the business and decided to reinvent their product. Their new approach was to reduce the size of the burger and lower the cost by selling it only one way: prewrapped, with ketchup, pickle, and onion dressings. They eliminated

Customers line up in front of the San Bernardino, California, hamburger stand opened in 1948 by Richard and Maurice McDonald. From this small stand grew the giant fast-food corporation McDonald's.

curb service, all dishes, and utensils.

On the day the McDonald's restaurant reopened in 1948, confused customers couldn't understand why no one was taking their orders, delivering food, or taking their trash away. It was a mess. But within several months people began to praise the 15-cent hamburgers and fast service. By 1951 McDonald's was selling a million hamburgers a year. The McDonald brothers began selling franchises. In 1961 businessman Ray Kroc bought out the McDonald brothers for $2 million.

In 1967 McDonald's raised the price of its hamburger to 18 cents, a day referred to in the national press as Black Wednesday. After 19 years of the 15-cent hamburger, prices would never be that low again.

The late 1960s and early 1970s were years of upheaval

in the United States. Traumatic events such as the Vietnam War, the assasination of Martin Luther King Jr., and the Watergate scandal left many people with doubts about their world. They began to question everything, from the politicians in Washington, D.C., to the food they ate.

Although McDonald's and Burger King had become popular in the 1950s and early 1960s by pioneering a way to produce cheap, fast food, people noticed that these hamburgers didn't taste the way individually made hamburgers had tasted in the coffee shops and restaurants of earlier days. The choice of what a customer wanted on a hamburger was gone. A person who wanted a quick hamburger had to eat whatever toppings had already been added. Even though the food was inexpensive and served quickly, many people missed being able to eat a custom-made hamburger.

Dave knew this because he missed those hamburgers as much as anyone else. "I just always loved hamburgers," Dave reminisces. "I loved them, and I still do, with mustard, pickle, and onion."

Dave had been a student of the perfect hamburger for many years. Back in his days as manager of the Hobby House, he and Richard Clauss would seek out good hamburger restaurants. They would sample the hamburgers and ask the owners questions about the ingredients and cooking processes. Dave had a lot of knowledge in his head. And not too surprisingly, Dave was bored with his job at Arthur Treacher's. He wanted to pursue his dream of creating the perfect hamburger restaurant.

Business friend Len Immke, who owned a car dealership in Columbus, enjoyed listening to Dave's "hamburger dreams." The two businessman both worked out at the Columbus Athletic Club. In the steam room Dave would regale Len with ideas for his future restaurant. One day the men decided to go to the club's dining room for a hamburger, but the restaurant was closed.

"See, Dave, it's what I've been telling you," Len said.

"It's tough to get a meal downtown at the noon hour. We really ought to have a hamburger operation down here."

Len knew the perfect spot for Dave's hamburger restaurant. A steak house owned by Tommy Heinrich, a former pro baseball player with the New York Yankees, had gone out of business. The building, at 257 East Broad Street in downtown Columbus, belonged to Len, who offered to rent the space to Dave for $250 a month. They shook hands that day, and Dave's hamburger restaurant was on its way.

Dave searched for a name that would be just right. His children's names appealed to him—Pam, Kenny, Molly, Melinda, and Lori—but somehow none was quite right for the name of a hamburger restaurant.

Former New York Yankees first baseman Tommy Heinrich owned a steak house in Columbus that had gone out of business. Dave decided to open his new restaurant in the building. He named it after his daughter Melinda Lou, who had been nicknamed "Wendy" by his other children.

Dave hit upon the name Wendy's in an unusual way: "When my daughter Melinda Lou was born, neither her brother nor her two sisters could pronounce her name. They started calling her Wenda, which then turned into Wendy."

With her red hair and freckles, Wendy Thomas had the wholesome, all-American look Dave was searching for. So he had an ad agency artist sketch out the logo for the restaurant, using Wendy as the model.

As an eight-year-old, Wendy was excited to be the namesake for her dad's new restaurant. "I remember Mom making a dress and then going down to a studio and putting my hair up in pigtails with that stuff that makes your hair stick straight out," she recalls. "I was sitting in a studio for a couple hours and smiling until I thought my mouth felt like it was going to fall off."

While preparation for opening the restaurant continued, Dave read story after story in business publications about how the fast-food market was too crowded, especially when it came to hamburger restaurants. So Dave offered up some extra prayers on the day Wendy's opened— November 15, 1969.

He need not have worried. On the first day, customers were lined up out the door and down the street. The opening party included the mayor of Columbus. And business never let up. Wendy's began making money after just six weeks in business. A year later, on November 21, 1970, Dave opened a second Wendy's on the outskirts of Columbus. This store featured a second grill just for orders that were placed at the drive-up window—a unique concept at the time.

As strange as it sounds, Dave was still working for Arthur Treacher's while overseeing the two Wendy's restaurants. Despite his success, Dave didn't feel confident enough to quit his job. But in 1971 Dave launched two more Wendy's restaurants in the Columbus area. Both stores opened to record sales of $10,000 a week. "We knew then that we really had something," Dave says. "It was no longer a matter of if we were going to make it, but how big it was going to be." Finally, he felt secure enough to leave his job at Arthur Treacher's to serve full-time as chairman of the board of Wendy's corporation.

Wendy's was finally the successful business Dave had envisioned. But being a success in business left little time for a family life. In the Thomas household Lorraine filled both the mother and the father roles for the couple's five children.

Pam, the oldest of the five Thomas kids, says her father missed an enormous part of their growing up. "My dad did not know where my high school was," she says. "I'm telling you he did not know where our schools were. He had never been to the parent-teacher conference, the awards banquets, or any of that."

In his 1994 book *Well Done!* Dave talks about the conflict of not having enough time to spend with his family when his kids were growing up:

> Could I have attended a few more school plays, spent a couple more days at the beach, or gone with the kids for a drive or two more and just chatted? Sure, I could have. But success is a funny thing. You make a commitment and you do it. In the world of earning a living, at least, you can never forget to factor in one very powerful truth: there are very few half-successful people.

In 1972 Wendy's was a full-blown success story. Keeping Wendy's successful would become Dave's next challenge.

Clara Peller delivered the most memorable line during the 1982 "hamburger war"
between Wendy's, McDonald's, and Burger King. In a television commercial, Peller asked
Wendy's competors, "Where's the beef?"

7

STAYING ON TRACK

WENDY'S WENT INTO business at a time when experts were saying that the fast-food industry was too crowded for any more newcomers. Even though Dave had read these warnings in business publications such as the *Wall Street Journal*, he found a way to make Wendy's successful by making his hamburgers different from the rest of the prewrapped burger sellers. In other words, he gave Wendy's its own identity.

Dave created the Wendy's hamburger with four features that he hoped would set it apart from the competition. First, the hamburger patty had to weigh a quarter of a pound. Both the size and shape of the patty were very important. "We designed the patty so that the edges would stick out over the sides of the bun," Dave explained. "That sent a message to people about how big it was—what Grandma Minnie said about not cutting corners."

Secondly, Dave used only fresh meat instead of frozen patties. He wanted to ensure that the sandwich tasted fresh, so the condiments were kept cold, and the hamburger patty did not touch the bun until the hamburger was sold. Only whole lettuce, not shredded lettuce, was

Today, drive-through business makes up about half of the sales in Wendy's.

used on Dave's hamburger.

Third, the hamburgers were made to order, not pre-cooked, and Dave offered a choice of eight toppings. This created 256 possible ways that a customer could order a hamburger at Wendy's.

Fourth, Dave was determined that customers would have an inviting place in which to eat the hamburger. "I wanted a building that had carpeting, and one where we didn't tell you to hurry up and get the heck out of there," Dave says.

After years of perfecting his own ability to grill a good hamburger, Dave decided that he would pass on this technique to all of the Wendy's grill people. The hamburger took four minutes to cook, but Dave wanted the customer to have it 15 seconds after it was ordered. So Dave set up a system. The grill person was trained to keep an eye on the door so that he or she knew about how many hamburgers needed to be grilling at any one time. The hamburgers that were cooked but not sold were crumbled up and used in Wendy's chili.

The best way to rankle Dave Thomas is to refer to Wendy's food as *fast food*. Dave hates the term because it was created to describe the prewrapped food that McDonald's pioneered. "We weren't and aren't a fast-food restaurant," Dave insists in his book *Dave's Way*. "Our service is fast. Our goal is to get the order to the customer in fifteen seconds at the counter and thirty seconds at the pick-up window. Our food is not cooked any faster or any slower than any other restaurant [food]."

An important part of every Wendy's restaurant is the drive-through window. Dave wanted to provide the same kind of carryout service that had worked so well with his Kentucky Fried Chicken stores. But the drive-through service was creating complaints. So in 1971 Dave gave new Wendy's president Bob Barney an assignment: make a pick-up window system that works right.

Bob went to work in a Wendy's restaurant in order to find out what was wrong. He quickly discovered that the main problem with getting food at the pick-up window was the microphone-speaker system. It worked properly only about half the time. Customers couldn't hear what the order takers were saying, and the order takers couldn't hear what the customers were saying.

Better microphones and speakers were installed. The sound quality was improved because there had been some recent breakthroughs in transistor technology. Bob also found that the speakers should be far enough away from the pick-up window so that three orders could be filled between the time an order was placed and when it was picked up.

Today drive-through sales make up nearly half of all the food sold in Wendy's restaurants. And the innovations that Bob created with the pick-up window have been copied over and over by the other fast-food chains. Dave is proud of his company's creation: "We have the best pick-up window in the business."

In August 1972, the first Wendy's franchise was sold. An entrepreneur named L. S. Hartzog purchased the rights to operate Wendy's restaurants in Indianapolis, Indiana. Dave was an innovator when it came to selling franchises. Rather than selling the rights to a single store, Dave would sell the franchise rights for an entire city or even part of a state. This helped the company grow quickly.

By the end of 1974, total sales at Wendy's restaurants were $25 million and net income was more than $1 million. Wendy's offices were getting 500 phone calls a week from people who wanted to buy a franchise. "People were saying, 'Dave, I hear you've got a new hamburger place. I want to come and see it,'" recalls Wendy's executive Ron Musick. "They would come and he would sell them a franchise that afternoon."

By 1975 the 100th Wendy's restaurant opened. After an incredible year of growth, on December 15, 1976, the company opened its 500th restaurant in Toronto, Canada. Wendy's was now an international company. Three months earlier, in September 1976, Wendy's had its first public stock offering, selling one million shares at $28 apiece.

Wendy's unprecedented rate of growth continued. Less than two-and-a-half years after opening its 500th store, the ribbon-cutting for Wendy's 1,500th store was held on March 20, 1979. This store was located in Puerto Rico. By November 15, 1979—exactly 10 years after the first Wendy's had opened—there were 1,767 stores in the United States, Puerto Rico, Canada, and Europe. During one 21-month period, 750 new Wendy's restaurants had opened—an incredible rate of more than a store per day.

Even Dave was impressed at the number of Wendy's restaurants that were popping up. "One year we opened 500 restaurants, and we really weren't capable of opening 500 restaurants," he says. "But we did it. It was really important to have those 500 restaurants, because it gave us national recognition that we could go on national TV."

Dave felt like he needed to build the chain quickly, because if Wendy's was large enough, he could afford the high cost of running a national advertising campaign. This would help Wendy's compete with the large chains, such as McDonald's and Burger King, that were driving hundreds of smaller competitors out of business. "We were moving like a jet plane down the runway—a thousand restaurants in one hundred months and the first hamburger chain to achieve $1 billion in sales in its first ten years."

By 1981 McDonald's, Burger King, and Wendy's were selling 60 percent of all hamburgers sold. All three companies realized that they were locked in a three-way battle for market share. *Market share* is a term for the number, or percentage, of all the consumers who buy the product you make.

The next year, Burger King launched what is now called "the Great Hamburger War of 1982." Instead of telling consumers why Burger King food was better, the management at Burger King decided to tell consumers what was wrong with McDonald's and Wendy's. Burger King commercials claimed that broiling hamburgers made them taste better than the frying method used at McDonald's or Wendy's. This advertising campaign cost $18 million, an enormous sum for advertising in those days.

When word leaked out that the advertisements would begin, McDonald's went to court to get a federal restraining order that would stop Burger King from running the commercials. But the request by McDonald's was denied and the commercials went on the air. Wendy's responded by offering to hold a national taste test to let the hamburger-buying public decide, but both of the other chains turned Dave down. Eventually McDonald's and Wendy's filed lawsuits to stop the advertisements. In its lawsuit McDonald's said Burger King's claim that its was the only burger that was broiled was false, because Burger King's hamburgers were reheated by microwave and steamed after they were cooked the first time.

In 1982, Burger King, the number-two hamburger chain in the United States, launched ads targeting its main competitors: McDonald's and Wendy's. When the restaurant chains responded with attack ads of their own, the "hamburger wars" were on.

The news media reported all the accusations flying back and forth, as well as people's opinions about the ethics of this style of advertising. A truce was called one month after the burger war was declared. All parties agreed to an out-of-court settlement. The terms of the agreement were that Burger King would stop its current series of commercials.

Burger King claimed that its tactics had resulted in a sales increase of 30 percent. But it was too soon for Burger King to gloat; the Great Hamburger War had only begun.

Dave wanted to tell people why Wendy's hamburgers were better, but in a humorous way. The hardest part of coming up with a new advertising slogan was to find a good message. At the time, Burger King had just reduced the amount of beef in its hamburger. Wendy's marketing executive Charles Rath says this event was the perfect opportunity to point out that "there was more bun than beef."

To sell this message, Wendy's hired a retired manicurist from Chicago named Clara Peller for a TV commercial. In the TV spot, Clara and two other elderly women are looking at an enormous hamburger bun. When the top is lifted off, a tiny hamburger is revealed. Clara then looks around and asks blankly, "Where's the beef?"

The way Dave explains it in his book *Dave's Way*, Clara Peller's delivery is what made the commercial funny and memorable. "Clara couldn't hear very well," Dave says. "So when it was time for her to deliver her lines, someone pinched her and she blurted out, 'Where's the beef?'"

The TV commercial was an overnight hit. "Where's the Beef?" became a household phrase. It popped up everywhere, from bumper stickers and cartoons to Sunday sermons and songs. The "Where's the Beef" line even got picked up during the 1984 presidential campaign. In a televised debate among the Democratic Party candidates, Walter Mondale used the slogan to suggest that Gary Hart had no substance to his ideas. "When I hear your new ideas," Mondale said, turning to Hart, "I'm reminded of that ad: Where's the beef?"

Wendy's sales skyrocketed 36 percent. Burger King announced that the Whopper would be changed to have more beef and less bun, but not because of the Wendy's campaign. Burger King said its own taste tests had revealed that the "customers had long indicated that there was too much bun and that perhaps they'd like more meat."

The burger wars have never really ended. "The ferocious battle for burger-bucks wages on, as periods of relative calm are followed by nasty price wars and cutthroat competition," Jeffrey Tennyson says in *Hamburger Heaven*. "As the burger superpowers continue aggressively to pursue an agenda of international expansion, the great American hamburger wars will undoubtedly, eventually, erupt into global conflict. It's only a matter of time."

Throughout the mid-1980s Wendy's continued to flourish. The Thomases' five children were grown, and Dave and Lorraine were spending time at their house in Florida. Dave learned to play golf and even bought a golf course.

But up north in Columbus, Ohio, Wendy's was struggling to stay successful. "Wendy's stock went from nearly $20 in 1984 and 1985 all the way down to about $4 a couple years later," says stockbroker Peter Oakes. "So investors had obviously lost their enthusiasm for the company at that point."

Wendy's had grown so fast that the corporation could not maintain the quality that Dave had insisted upon for each restaurant. Customers complained and some stores closed.

In the beginning, explains Wendy's marketing executive Don Calhoon, "all we had to do was open up restaurants and the people came. We didn't have any national television at that point. They just came. Today it's very much a share battle. If one company wins, it's because somebody else is losing."

With so much at stake Wendy's needed Dave Thomas back on the job. After the success of Clara Peller's commercials, Wendy's was looking for a celebrity spokesperson who truly loved Wendy's food. Wendy's executive Ron Musick says that after looking for the right celebrity spokesperson, they realized that person was Dave Thomas. In 1989 Dave began appearing in Wendy's commercials. "More than anything I'm a marketer," Dave says "I love to sell."

"One day I went to the [advertising] agency and spent six hours explaining how we make hamburgers fresh and cook them to order," Dave remembers. "I guess I was preaching, but you could see that I believed what I was saying."

In Wendy's TV commercials, Dave says, the writers put in his style of humor to sell the product: "I don't like gourmet restaurants, putting on airs. I like short-sleeved shirts. I like good food and good hamburgers."

Since 1989, Dave Thomas has appeared in more than 500 commercials for Wendy's. But is Dave the happy-go-lucky hamburger guy he portrays in the commercials? No,

Today, Wendy's doesn't need celebrities to sell its hamburgers and other products; Dave himself is the corporation's main pitchman.

says his daughter Pam. "He's not like that. That's the myth, that he's lighthearted and real funny," she told A&E's *Biography*. "People put him on a pedestal, and they think he knows everything. He's not; he's just a person. He's had a tough life and he's made the best of it. He doesn't complain about it."

With all the success that Dave Thomas enjoyed as the founder and spokesperson of Wendy's, some people might have guessed that all of his troubles were behind him. But Dave would still face a few more challenges in the years ahead.

Dave Thomas speaks to Congress in 1995. While work takes up a great amount of Dave's time, he also devotes a lot of his time and money to good causes, such as adoption and cancer research.

8

DAVE TODAY

THE 5,000TH WENDY'S restaurant opened on March 27, 1997, in Pickering, Ohio, a suburb of Columbus. "I opened the first Wendy's restaurant because I felt there was a place for fresh hamburgers made just the way the customer wants," Dave said at the ribbon-cutting ceremony. "That's as true today as it was 27 years ago."

Today there are Wendy's restaurants in 32 countries. The corporation has benefitted as well from its 1995 merger with Tim Horton's, a Canadian chain of restaurants that feature coffee, baked goods, soup, and deli-style sandwiches. Dave Thomas is a wealthy, successful businessman who stars in his own commercials.

But Dave has not forgotten the hardships of his early years, and he spends countless hours supporting a variety of worthy causes. "I believe everyone has an obligation to put back into life more than what they take out," Dave says in his autobiography. "People who are successful have the biggest responsibility because along with the money they have the name and contacts to do the most good."

It is hard to imagine that someone as successful and generous as

Dave Thomas would feel insecure about anything in life. But growing up poor and neglected is a hard thing to forget. "Off and on for years I've found myself laying awake nights worrying about being poor again. I think about it a lot because I remember the days I didn't have anything or anyone. I don't know if I can ever relax and say 'I have so much I can stop worrying now.'"

Dave also grew up feeling embarrassed about the shortcomings in his past. "There were three things I never wanted anyone to know about me: being born out of wedlock, being adopted, and quitting school," Dave told A&E's *Biography*. "I had nothing to do with the first two, but quitting school was one of the most stupid mistakes I made."

Dave is often asked to give speeches about the value of education. But back in the early 1990s students asked Dave the same question over and over again: If you believe in education so much, why don't you go back and get your high school diploma?

Not being a person to dodge a challenge, Dave told Lorraine he wanted to get his General Equivalency Diploma (GED). She urged him to go for it. Coconut Creek High School, near Fort Lauderdale, Florida, "adopted" Dave. Then he set about hiring a tutor and preparing for the six-hour test.

"He finally took it and he passed it," Lorraine says, her voice filled with pride. "I read that test. And I think if I had to take that thing today, I don't think I could make it."

On March 25, 1993, Dave Thomas received his GED as an honorary graduate of Coconut Creek High School. Dave was voted "Most Likely to Succeed" in his class. More than 40 years after the senior year he never had, Dave and Lorraine were named honorary king and queen of the prom.

"Before we went to the prom that night, my son, Kenny, called me and told me to have a good time but to be home by ten," Dave recalls. "Wise guy—just like his old man."

When Dave lists his most important priorities in life, he tops that list with his wife, Lorraine, their five children, and their 14 grandchildren. And yet he does not dispute that, like many ambitious fathers, he was an absentee parent for most of his children's childhood.

"I have to confess that I cheated my kids by not being involved enough in raising them," Dave writes in *Dave's Way*. "You see, I didn't give them a very good idea of what a father should be like, so that when they raised their own children, they didn't have a model to look back on. Despite this, my four married kids do pretty well splitting up the job of raising children between husband and wife. So Lorraine—again—may have succeeded in doing the work for both of us."

Dave concedes that he has more time now to listen to

Lorraine Thomas helps her husband prepare for his graduation ceremony. Forty-five years after dropping out of high school, Dave Thomas earned his General Equivalency Diploma, proudly graduating from Coconut Creek High School in 1993.

his kids and see their points of view. But he is proud of the fact that he never worried about spoiling his kids. "They are my kids, and if they are spoiled by my giving and can't handle it, that's their problem."

He wishes he had pushed his kids harder to get their college degrees, but he never wanted to burden his kids with his ambitions. He was always more interested that they brought home the right attitude than an A report card.

Even so, he says he wants his grandchildren to get good educations. "A good education gives a person more self-confidence," Dave says. "I've always had to fight for everything, and I think that with an education you don't have to fight quite so hard. You have more choices open to you, and you can choose without as much fear of failure."

Those who know Dave say he expects from others what he expects from himself. With someone as driven to success as Dave Thomas, his expectations of others can loom large. "He has a sixth sense," says his son, Ken. "When he asks you a question, he already knows the answer. He wants to know if you know the answer. He does that quite a bit with people, especially me. I don't call it entrapment, but it's pretty darn close to it."

As with any large family of independent thinkers, especially those who came of age in the 1960s, the Thomas family has had its share of differences with one another. But there is an obvious strand of love and caring that threads its way through the stories Dave tells about his family's conflicts.

One chapter in *Dave's Way* is entitled "Never Harass Anybody You Don't Like." Dave writes: "The Wendy's TV ads make me seem like a nice guy, and I try to be. Most of the time. But I'm also tough on people in a quiet kind of way. If you are going to serve the customer right, that means you have to run a tight ship. Sometimes you have to be tough on people to do that the right way."

Dave jokingly refers to his management style as harass-ment—and he says he perfected this technique on his chil-

Shawna and Zamara Grant get a suprise visit from Dave Thomas at Shands Children's Hospital in Florida. Dave was at the hospital in May 1999 to make a donation to the Children's Miracle Network.

dren. One year when his kids were squabbling, he called them and told them to meet him at the restaurant for a nice Christmas lunch. If one of them was missing, Dave warned, no one got anything for Christmas. Although they moaned and groaned, they all showed up. The family talked out some differences they had over lunch.

"You may call it manipulation," Dave writes. "I prefer to call it constructive bribery. I reminded them they would all stick together when the chips were down, even if they squabbled once in a while. It was worth it. They gave me a card that said, 'Harassment is the family form of love in the Thomas home.'"

Dave's stick-together lesson paid off in 1990. Dave and

his daughter Wendy were in Chicago for a large company meeting when Dave suddenly became violently ill with nausea and vomiting. He canceled his presentation and flew back to Columbus, where he was admitted to the hospital.

By his own admission this was a bad time to be seriously sick. Lorraine, his two daughters Pam and Lori, and his daughter-in-law, Kathy, were all traveling together in Italy. Molly was off in northern Michigan. Wendy was in Chicago giving the presentation Dave should have given. Ken and Dave were angry with each other and not speaking.

But with a crisis unfolding the Thomas family mobilized like an efficient field army called into battle. When Wendy heard her dad was in the hospital and that the doctor wanted to operate, she flew from Chicago to Columbus immediately. "I can still remember her pacing the linoleum floor with a handheld cellular phone in the corridor outside my room, trying to 'Buona sera!' her way through the Italian switchboards to get in touch with Lorraine," Dave recalls.

The powerful father, accustomed to running the show as head of a major American restaurant corporation, was now looking to his daughter for strength. It was an unforgettable moment for Dave: "She spent some quality time with dear old dad, telling him that it was going to be okay and that it was just a question of having the right mental attitude. But dear old dad was scared to death—frightened about what the doctors were going to do to him."

By the time Dave was ready to go under anesthesia,

WHY ADOPTION IS IMPORTANT

In his book *Dave's Way*, Dave made this list of five reasons why he feels adoption is important:

1. There are kids who are growing up living in makeshift orphanages made out of converted office space and worse in some parts of this country. That shouldn't happen in the most powerful country in the world.

2. Without a home and affection, the chances for making it in this world are mighty slim.

3. Children raised out of homes often end up in trouble and as burdens to society.

4. If you have had the blessing of a good home life yourself, then you do owe something back.

5. The world works on families—it really does. Don't let fear stop you from being an adoptive parent.

Molly had found a charter flight to Columbus, Ken was on his way to the hospital, and the rest of the Thomas family was scurrying back from Italy. Wendy and Molly were there as Dave was about to receive anesthesia. Kenny arrived just as they wheeled him down to the operating room. Dave grabbed his hand and said, "Glad you're here, my boy."

After a four-hour operation doctors removed a non-cancerous tumor located between Dave's large intestine and liver. "I learned some lessons from the whole experience," Dave reflects. "That Wendy was right to bring the family together. That the family was right to come together and to share in making a big decision (it made us stronger and helped heal a few people-to-people wounds). And that cancer research is a pretty good area to support charitably." One of Dave's favorite causes— both before and after his emergency operation—is the Arthur James Cancer Research Institute at Ohio State University in Columbus.

Richard Clauss has been friends with Dave since their working days at the Hobby House Restaurant in Fort Wayne. After Dave became rich and successful, Richard says he asked Dave if there was anything he still wanted out of life that he hadn't done yet. "What he told me just floored me," Clauss says. "He said his greatest desire was to lose 40 pounds."

Even though Dave had always been active, his weight had steadily crept up on him. Late one Saturday night in 1996 Dave awakened Lorraine with some bad news. He told her he couldn't breathe—and then he collapsed.

She called the emergency medical service, and Dave was taken to the hospital. Doctors there told Dave he had had a massive heart attack. He nearly died that night. "God threw him back because he had more to do," Lorraine says. "He didn't want him yet. That's what it's all about. So he's still here with us."

Never one to waste a good lesson in life, Dave made a quick recovery and then shared his experience with others by making a public service commercial promoting the use of 911. He also got his wish: Dave lost more than 40 pounds, and he is more conscious of what he eats these days. "Believe it or not, I eat more red meat today than I did before my heart attack," Dave says. "But it is in moderation."

But aside from his support of cancer research and his advocacy of eating right, Dave directs a lot of his attention to adoption programs.

Dave admits that he was once embarrassed about being adopted. Even after he was successful, when he gave a motivational talk to Wendy's managers, he would sometimes neglect to mention that part of his background. In his book *Well Done!* Dave tells about the experience that made him see the importance of promoting adoption: "One day a young African-American manager buttonholed me and said, 'Dave, when you gave your speech today, you left out the part about being adopted. Why did you do that? I always related to that because I was adopted myself.'"

Dave realized that he had been avoiding his true feelings about being adopted. Now when he talks to an audience about doing the right thing or about taking responsibility in life, he asks two questions: "How many of you remember the father and mother who gave birth to you? How many of you never met the father and mother who gave birth to you?" When Dave raises his hand and several people in the audience join him in raising their hands, Dave says he feels proud to be "out of the closet."

In 1990 Dave was asked by former president George Bush to be the national spokesperson for a program called "Adoption Works . . . for Everyone." In 1992 Dave established the Dave Thomas Foundation for Adoption. He created the foundation in order to make people aware of the thousands of children in this country who need permanent homes and loving families. The foundation promotes employee benefit programs to make it easier for working parents to adopt children.

Dave signs copies of his 1994 book Well Done! *He donated all the proceeds from this book to benefit adoption programs, just as he did with the autobiography he published three years earlier,*

Every November all Wendy's restaurants in the United States promote adoption through restaurant displays, posters, and tray liners (protective sheets of paper used on food trays). The foundation has published a pamphlet called "The Beginner's Guide to Adoption" to help people who are interested in adoption. Dave supports his foundation with the profits from his two books, *Dave's Way* and *Well Done!* and with annual fund-raising events.

According to Dave's foundation, there are more than 100,000 children in the public child welfare system who want to be adopted. Older kids, those from minority cultures, siblings who want to be adopted together, and kids with physical or mental challenges are often hard to place with families. But Dave believes that no child is "unadoptable."

With more than 5,000 restaurants in 32 countries, including this one in Madrid, Spain, Wendy's is one of the largest restaurant chains in the world.

In July of 1998 the Dave Thomas Foundation for Adoption and Capital University Law School, Columbus, established the Dave Thomas Center for Adoption Law. The Thomas Center is the first university-based center in the country that specializes in adoption law.

Thomas Center director Kent Markus says that Dave Thomas's popularity and financial support for the cause of adoption is wonderful. But it is Dave's passion for the cause that has made his efforts such a success.

Dave has also lobbied Congress to get major adoption reform laws passed by Congress. In 1995, he testified before the House Ways and Means Committee, urging the committee to support a tax credit for parents who adopt a child. When the tax credit was signed into law the next year, President Bill Clinton credited Dave for his work with adopted children. In 1997, Dave was invited to the White House for a bill-signing ceremony after the passage of additional legislation that he had supported. Among other improvements, the new law signed by Clinton works to get children out of a perpetual foster-care system and into permanent, stable adoptive homes.

"[Dave Thomas has] played an important role in getting people to put politics aside and find the common ground that makes things happen in Washington," Markus says.

The Thomas Center wants to promote adoption by focusing on education, advocacy, and research. "We are offering the first-ever class at an American law school exclusively dedicated to adoption law," Markus says. "We will take the course material and then send it out to law schools across the country to encourage family law professors to offer an adoption law course."

At an academic symposium held at the Thomas Center, First Lady Hillary Clinton spoke in a videotape about Dave's commitment to helping make adoption possible for more children: "Dave Thomas, there is no one in America who has done more for the cause of adoption than you have."

As director of the Thomas Center, Markus works with the staffs of key congressional representatives to provide guidance for future adoption laws on the federal level and for helping other states design their laws to comply with the 1997 federal law. The Thomas Center provides special adoption law expertise when an adoption law matter is called into court. The center also has a partnership with the American Trial Lawyers Association to recruit lawyers from around the country to provide free legal services that

As he looks toward the future, Dave Thomas continues to work hard and give both time and money generously.

will help children be adopted.

"We've got a recruitment effort to encourage lawyers to help out and be part of the solution instead of part of the problem," Markus says. In the area of research, Markus says that the center will join forces with a university school of social sciences to do research on the critical issues of adoption. "We're doing research about the problems, what are the roadblocks and how might those roadblocks be moved out of the way," Markus explains. "Where might we modify the legal system in order to make it easier for kids to get through to adoption while still protecting everybody's rights. Those are the research questions we want to explore."

In his book *Dave's Way*, Dave explains why adoption

has become such an important cause in his life: It may sound strange to you that I should support adoption, because my adopted childhood was not all that happy. That's not the way I look at it. Adoption made it possible for me to get Minnie Sinclair's love and teaching. Adoption gave me my adoptive mother's care and affection in my early years, even if I don't remember it. And although he had different values than I grew up to believe in, my adoptive father tried his best. Had I not been adopted, I could have ended up as a ward of the state or raised in a county orphanage. So the way I see it, adoption turned out to be a big plus for me.

When his own children were grown, with families of their own, they began to ask Dave about his birth father. They needed a family medical history for their children's school applications. Eventually Dave found out who his birth father was.

Dave's oldest daughter, Pam, began by checking the Philadelphia area for information about the name listed on Dave's birth certificate as his father. She found the wife of one of the man's cousins. Although Dave's birth father, Sam, had died years before Pam's call, the Thomas family decided to go to Philadelphia and meet some of Sam's relatives.

Dave learned that Sam had been a stockbroker who was single until he was 35 years old. He had a son who is a college professor. No one in Sam's family was familiar with Dave's birth mother. It was possible, they said, that Sam never knew about Dave being born.

■   ■   ■

What's next for Dave Thomas? Dave says he intends to keep making TV commercials for Wendy's "as long as I'm having a good time. When I stop having a good time and having fun, I'll stop. I don't know when that's going to be. I've got a dual message: selling hamburgers and chicken sandwiches at Wendy's, and adoption. After I do commercials, I use TV to talk about adoption and education."

The man who dropped out of high school in 10th grade now holds honorary degrees from Duke, Baylor, Clemson, and several other universities. Once told by his father that he would never amount to anything, Dave Thomas in 1979 received the prestigious Horatio Alger Award, an annual award given to an outstanding individual who has succeeded despite great adversity. But despite the many examples of success in his life, Dave Thomas is not ready to put up his feet and take it easy. "Because I always have kept moving, my life today is both happy and dissatisfied. I wouldn't have it any other way," Dave says in his autobiography. "In a way, my achievements were made easier by having such a rootless life in my early years. Had I grown up on a street in a small town with a set of family and friends, there would have been the temptation to sit back, relax, and enjoy life. As it was, there was nothing to hold me back from looking for more."

The bottom line, according to Dave, is to know yourself well enough not to get carried away with all the luxuries of life. "Everybody has toys—things we buy to give us pleasure—and they're OK within reason. But you have to make sure you own the toys, and not vice versa." Dave has called one of his own "toys" his "most stupid purchase." He once bought a multi-million dollar yacht because he had wanted to own a boat ever since the day his father took him for a boat ride on Gull Lake in Michigan. However, Dave soon realized the enormous expense of keeping a crew of four seamen to run and maintain the boat was a mistake. "One year after buying it the sheer stupidity of the expense got the better of me," he says. "It wasn't that I couldn't afford it. It was why I needed to. So I sold the yacht to a business associate of mine. In a short time, he realized that he was just paying for misery, too. I'm glad I had the experience of owning a yacht, but reckless spending is not in my blood."

When a reporter asked Dave what he wanted to be remembered for, Dave told him, "That's not one of my major concerns in life. I'm not sure I want to be remembered. I mean, if I'm dead, why would I care about it anyway? I'd rather be remembered while I'm living."

Dave Thomas continues to create a living legacy of hard work and generosity for worthwhile causes. The adoption foundation he created and the financial backing he contributes to it are a fitting testimonial to a man who never forgot what it was like to be 13 years old and yearning for a stable home and loving, supportive parents.

"If you're not giving of yourself as much as you're giving of your wallet, are you really generous down deep?" Dave asks in *Well Done!* "We should work hard to make the virtuous circle of generosity the number one epidemic in the United States—giving of wealth, giving of self. Unstoppable and unending."

In 1990 Dave Thomas told a reporter for the *New York Times*, "If I can get just one child a home, it would be better than selling a million hamburgers." The extraordinary thing about Dave Thomas is that he has done both.

CHRONOLOGY

1932	R. David Thomas born in Atlantic City, New Jersey; adopted by Rex and Auleva Thomas of Kalamazoo, Michigan
1937	Adoptive mother, Auleva, dies of rheumatic fever
1938–42	As a boy, spends summers with Grandma Minnie Sinclair
1944	Begins working 12-hour shifts at the Regas Restaurant in Knoxville, Tennessee
1947	Thomas family moves to Fort Wayne. Dave gets a job at the Hobby House Restaurant
1950	Joins the army and trains at Cook and Baker School; during the next two years, serves in Germany as mess sergeant and manages the Enlisted Men's Club
1953	Returns to the Hobby House Restaurant job and meets Lorraine Buskirk
1954	Marries Lorraine Buskirk
1955	Meets Colonel Harland Sanders; With Phil Clauss, begins selling Kentucky Fried Chicken
1962	With family, moves to Columbus, Ohio, to run four ailing Kentucky Fried Chicken restaurants
1968	Sells his now-successful Kentucky Fried Chicken restaurants to the KFC Corporation and becomes a millionaire at age 35
1969	Quits job as Kentucky Fried Chicken regional director; opens the first Wendy's restaurant in downtown Columbus, Ohio, on November 15
1970	Opens second Wendy's restaurant on November 21
1972	Sells first Wendy's franchise, in Indianapolis, Indiana, to L. S. Herzog; founds Wendy's Management Institute in December as a place to train future restaurant managers
1976	First public offering of Wendy's stock, at $28 per share, held in September; Wendy's expands into Canada, opening 500th restaurant in Toronto on December 15
1978	Wendy's 1,000th restaurant opens
1979	Wendy's 1,500th restaurant opens in Puerto Rico; the 10th anniversary of Wendy's is celebrated in November with 1,767 restaurants worldwide
1980	Wendy's 2,000th restaurant opens on November 15

1981	Wendy's stock lists on the New York Stock Exchange for the first time (stock ticker symbol: WEN)
1982	Wendy's enters the "Great Hamburger War"; advertising slogan "Where's the Beef?" becomes a part of popular culture
1983	Wendy's 2, 500th restaurant opens in Silver Spring, Maryland
1985	Wendy's 3,000th restaurant opens in New Orleans's historic French Quarter on February 6
1990	Asked by President George Bush to be national spokesperson for the "Adoption Works . . . For Everyone" campaign
1991	Autobiography *Dave's Way* hits bookstores in September; Dave embarks on a national book tour, and donates proceeds from the book to national adoption awareness programs
1992	Wendy's 4,000th restaurant opens in Bentonville, Arkansas; Dave establishes the Dave Thomas Foundation for Adoption
1993	Receives his high school equivalency diploma (GED) from Coconut Creek High School and is voted "Most Likely to Succeed."
1994	Publishes second book, *Well Done!*, a collection of success stories, and once again donates proceeds from the book to national adoption programs; Wendy's celebrates 25th anniversary on November 15, with nearly 4,400 restaurants in 34 countries bringing in record sales
1995	Wendy's merges with Canadian chain Tim Horton's
1996	Suffers a heart attack, recovers, and begins doing public service announcements that promote the practice of calling 911
1997	Wendy's 5,000th restaurant opens in Pickering, Ohio, on March 27
1999	Attends ceremony in March as the U.S. Postal Service unveils a new stamp celebrating adoption

FURTHER READING

Egerton, Thomas, Christopher. *How to Open and Run a Successful Restaurant.* 2nd ed. New York: John Wiley & Sons, 1994.

Gordon, Robert T., and Mark H. Brezinski. *The Complete Restaurant Management Guide.* Armonk, N.Y.: M. E. Sharpe, 1999.

Kroc, Ray, with Robert Anderson. *Grinding It Out: The Making of McDonald's.* New York: St. Martin's Press, 1990.

McDonald, Ronald L. *The Complete Hamburger: The History of America's Favorite Sandwich.* Seacaucus, N.J.: Birch Lane Press, 1997.

Tennyson, Jeffrey. *Hamburger Heaven: The Illustrated History of the Hamburger.* New York: Warner Books, 1995.

Thomas, R. David. *Dave's Way: A New Approach to Old-Fashioned Success.* New York: Putnam, 1991.

Thomas, Dave, with Ron Beyma. *Well Done! The Common Guy's Guide to Everyday Success.* Grand Rapids, Mich.: Zondervan, 1994.

APPENDIX

ADOPTION ORGANIZATIONS

Adoption Advocates
328 W. Mistletoe
San Antonio, TX 78212
Phone: 210-734-4470
Fax: 210-734-5966
E-mail: adoption@netxpress.com

Adoption ARC
4701 Pine Street, no. J-7
Philadelphia, PA 19143
Phone: 215-748-1441
Fax: 215-842-9881
E-mail: Taralaw@aol.com

Adoption Resource Center
of Connecticut, Inc.
2389 Main Street
Glastonbury, CT 06033
Phone: 860-657-2626
Fax: 860-657-1304
E-mail: info@arcct.org

Adoption Service
Information Agency (A.S.I.A.)
7720 Alaska Avenue NW
Washington, DC 20012
Phone: 202-726-7193
Fax: 202-722-4928
E-mail: dcinfo@asia-adopt.org

Adoptive Families of America
2309 Como Avenue
St. Paul MN 55108
Phone: 651-645-9955
Fax: 651-645-0055
E-mail: adoptionop@aol.com

Angels' Haven Outreach
370 W. Grand Street, no. 207
Corona, CA 91720
Phone: 909-735-5400
Fax: 909-371-0161
E-mail: Sherry@angels-haven.com

Children at Heart Adoption Services
145 N. Main Street
Mechanicville, NY 12118
Phone: 518-664-5988
Fax: 518-664-1220
E-mail: info@childrenatheart.com

Dave Thomas Foundation
for Adoption
PO Box 7164
Dublin, OH 43017
Phone: 614-764-3009
Fax: 614-764-6707

The Family Network
307 Webster Street
Monterey, CA 93940
Phone: 408-655-5077
E-mail: geofamnet@aol.com

Holt International
Children's Services
1195 City View
Eugene, OR 97402
Phone: 541-687-2202
Fax: 541-683-6175
E-mail: info@hotintl.org

INDEX

PICTURE CREDITS

NANCY PEACOCK is the author of two Chelsea House books for young adults. She has also written articles and columns for *BusinessWeek*, *New Choices*, *Midwest Living*, *Romantic Homes*, *Cleveland Magazine*, and many other periodicals, as well as travel books and a historical fiction novel. She lives in Medina, Ohio with her husband Larry and two children, Aaron and Natalie.

JAMES SCOTT BRADY serves on the board of trustees with the Center to Prevent Handgun Violence and is the vice chairman of the Brain Injury Foundation. Mr. Brady served as assistant to the president and White House press secretary under President Ronald Reagan. He was severely injured in an assassination attempt on the president, but remained the White House press secretary until the end of the administration. Since leaving the White House, Mr. Brady has lobbied for stronger gun laws. In November 1993, President Bill Clinton signed the Brady Bill, a national law requiring a waiting period on handgun purchases and a background check on buyers.